D0540600

▲ *Top Prize Winning design in our 30th birthday Radio Times cover competition by Alice Roberts, aged fourteen, from Bristol.*

Biddy Baxter, Edward Barnes and **Lewis Bronze** devised and wrote the **Blue Peter Book**

This edition published by Ringpress Books, by arrangement with BBC Books, a division of BBC Enterprises Ltd. Blue Peter is a registered trade mark of the British Broadcasting Corporation.

Distributed by Ruskin Book Services Ltd., Unit 306, Hartlebury Trading Estate, Hartlebury, Kidderminster, Worcestershire DY10 4JB. Telephone (0299) 251505.

Hello There! from Blue Peter

And welcome to our 24th Blue Peter Book.

It's an important one because it celebrates 30 years of Blue Peter!

If you *really* stop and think about it – it makes you breathless. Two thousand, three hundred and seventeen programmes, over twenty-three thousand different items, sixteen presenters, fifteen pets, twenty-six Appeals, twenty-three foreign expeditions and millions and *millions* of letters!!

That means there are millions of Blue Peter badge winners, too, and if you've been lucky enough to win a badge, you'll know it comes with a very special bonus. There are now nearly sixty places – like exhibitions, theme parks or historic houses – where Blue Peter badge winners can get in free of charge. The list arrives with your badge, and with the huge increase in entrance fees, it's a bonus that's well worth having – so if you're on an outing – don't forget to take your badge!

By the time you read this, you may have seen the Radio Times' Blue Peter 30th Birthday Cover, designed by fourteen year old Alice Roberts of Bristol and there are some of the other prize

How many of these pictures can you identify?
Turn to page 76 for the answers!

1

winning designs by viewers who entered our competition at the beginning and the end of this book.

The saddest news of the past year was the death of one of Blue Peter's greatest friends – Percy Thrower. Percy had looked after our garden at Television Centre for fourteen years. He designed our Italian Sunken Garden and had taught presenters and viewers alike not only how to grow flowers and vegetables but how to get a great deal of pleasure from something very

2

3

4

simple – a small plot of earth. There's a tribute to Percy on page 27 of this book and photographs of Chris Crowder, who's taken over from him.

Another newcomer is Jet, our new pony for handicapped riders. He was provided as a result of our very successful Rags Appeal which also gave help to each one of the Riding for the Disabled's 635 Groups. You can catch up on Jet's progress on page 30.

It's also the very first time Yvette's been featured in a Blue Peter book – she arrived just too late for book 23. And what with Showjumping with Harvey Smith, White Water rafting and canoeing and bob sleighing to name but a few of her exploits, her feet haven't touched the ground since she joined the programme! Don't miss Yvette's Database on page 16, or the story of Yvette and Bonnie at Agility Classes on page 56.

Caron's year's been action-packed, too – quite often suspended in mid-air dangling on the end of a rope. And when she abseiled down Holyhead's South Stack, to help the RSPB fix a bird-spotting TV camera on the rock face, there was the added hazard of the turbulent waves of the Irish Sea directly below! That adventure's on page 18.

There are some of the year's most popular

'makes' in this book – and if you're a fan of Chef Curry (funny how something always goes wrong, when he's in the kitchen!) don't miss his mouth-watering Rigatoni Chicken on page 54.

But the highlight of the year must be last Summer's Expedition to the USSR. There are souvenir photos and a flashback to magic moments like Caron and Yvette's performance with the Moscow State Circus on page 38. And if you enjoy Blue Peter's Expeditions to foreign countries, write and tell us which part of the world you'd like us to explore next – you never know it may be *your* idea that's featured in Book 25!

BONNIE

WILLOW

GEORGE

MARK

CARON X

YVETTE

30 YEARS OF Blue Peter

1958 –
Christopher Trace and
Leila Williams were the
first Blue Peter presenters.
In 1988 it's Mark, Caron
and Yvette!

It is October 1958. The scene is the newly opened BBC Television Centre.

A Motor Scooter drives in ridden by a girl called Gillian Reilly who is a Television Producer's Assistant. A friend waves to her.

"What are you working on these days, Gillie?

"Blue Peter," she replies as she roars to a halt.

"What the heck's Blue Peter?"

"It's a sort of magazine programme … for children" She parks the scooter and runs upstairs to the office where her producer is very busy, playing trains on a full sized model railway layout.

The producer was not Biddy Baxter but a large Billy Bunterish looking man called John Hunter Blair. John loved trains and dolls. So he put together an idea for a programme for children aged between five and eight featuring a young actor

Editor Biddy Baxter with
Petra and Jason.

Valerie Singleton joined the programme in 1962 – the year Petra was born. Petra was a dog for all the viewers and took part in 1,192 editions of Blue Peter. When she died in 1977 viewers sent donations for a bronze statue by the sculptor William Timym, to be made in her memory.

PETRA
1962
1977

The Blue Peter Appeals began in 1962 with this toy collection. There's been one every Christmas – helping good causes at home and abroad.

The 1979 Great Blue Peter Bring & Buy Sale helped millions of starving Cambodians – victims of Pol Pot's cruel regime. The idea behind the Appeals wasn't just to raise money, but to tell viewers about people who were worse off than themselves and show them how they could help.

called Christopher Trace, playing with trains, and a very pretty former Miss Great Britain, called Leila Williams, playing with dolls. The programme was to be fifteen minutes long, once weekly, for a run of eight weeks. It opened to the tune of "Barnacle Bill", the same as today with the blue and white Blue Peter flag being raised on a three masted schooner. This signified the ship was about to leave port, like the programme, on a voyage of adventure. No one guessed how far that ship would sail!

But tragedy struck before the voyage had hardly begun. In the early Sixties John Hunter Blair died, and the programme he loved very nearly died with him.

In 1962 a whirlwind blew in from Broadcasting House, in the shape of Biddy Baxter. She quickly got together a new team and within a year they created the Blue Peter which you would recognise today.

OUT went the annual review of toys on sale for Christmas. "It's like a long boring commercial," they said.

IN came an Appeal asking children to send toys for other children who were too poor to have toys of their own. Christmas isn't just about getting. Why should children be denied the pleasure of giving? This was the first Blue Peter Appeal.

IN came the Blue Peter badge, which was to be *won* and worn with pride. No one was ever *given* a badge, to get one viewers had to write an interesting letter or send an idea for the programme. Biddy Baxter sometimes offended high and important people by refusing to *give* them badges for their children!

On the Christmas Programme of 1962 a large box tied up with pink ribbon appeared in the Blue Peter studio. Chris Trace untied the ribbon, and out popped Petra – the Blue Peter Dog. Petra was to appear in every programme. She was brought up and trained before the eyes of millions of viewers.

In 1964 Blue Peter held its first Guide Dog Appeal. Altogether the programme has puppy walked three Guide Dogs and provided funds to train another thirty-five, as well as building kennels, dogs' hospitals and Training Centres throughout the country. Puppy Walking Manager Derek Freeman chose all the Blue Peter pups.

She was a dog for everyone, because although every child would like a dog, only the lucky ones have a dog of their own. When Petra died in 1977 viewers sent in donations, asking for a statue to be erected in her honour. A large bronze head was commissioned from the sculptor William Timym, which now stands in the Blue Peter Garden.

In 1964 the Appeal was for viewers to collect a huge quantity of silver paper and milk bottle tops which was sold to buy

Expedition to Borneo, 1966 – presenter Val Singleton was the first white woman the local people had seen.

Expedition to Malaysia, 1980 – Sarah Greene at a snake farm. Blue Peter has visited every continent and sub continent in the world!

and train Honey, the first Blue Peter Guide Dog. The Appeal also gave the programme two lasting friendships. Elsie Whitehead became the first owner of Honey, and later, when Honey retired, of Buttons, the second Blue Peter Guide Dog. Elsie and her dogs have been regular visitors to the studio for nearly 25 years. Derek Freeman, a Yorkshireman was the Puppy Walking Manager for Guide Dogs for the Blind. Derek's bounding enthusiasm, his deep concern for blind people and his love of dogs were all so abundant on Television that viewers took him to their hearts. He has featured in hundreds of programmes over a quarter of a century, and during that time has passed on more knowledge and common sense about the training of dogs than anyone else on television.

Blue Peter went twice-weekly in 1964, and began to be the most watched children's programme in Britain. It soon became obvious that two presenters were not enough to cope with the double demands of making two programmes a week, so the hunt for a third member of the team was on.

Biddy Baxter saw a photograph of a young actor in her local paper *The Leicester Mercury*, and said, "He's got a cheeky expression … let's get him in and have a chat with him." His name was John Noakes.

John joined the programme in 1966 and rapidly became the delight of the viewers and the despair of the production team. John was young and fresh and

Presenter John Noakes' most embarrassing moment – when he forgot the name of comedian Ronnie Barker, leading this unusual bike team! John was amazingly brave – he once climbed to the top of Nelson's Column to clean the Admiral's hat!

Shep became as popular as John. He even had a song written about him.

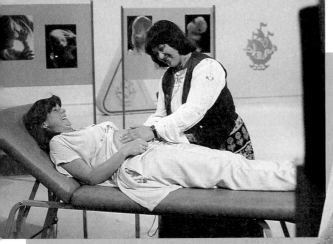

Tina Heath was the first Blue Peter presenter to become pregnant. Viewers heard baby Jemma's heart beats before she was born!

amazingly brave; climbing up a flimsy ladder to the top of Nelson's Column was just one of his feats of derring-do. But when it came to appearing in the studio on a live programme, he couldn't remember a line or a name, or what he was supposed to do next.

Once Ronnie Barker was making a surprise visit to the studio to support one of his local charities. John introduced him by saying, "And this you will have no difficulty in recognising as Ronnie-er Ronnie-Ronnie ..."

"Corbett?" interjected Barker.

"That's right ... No it isn't, is it?"

Viewers loved his mistakes as much as his dares. He took over one of Petra's puppies, called Patch, and after Patch died he had a sheepdog called Shep. John and the dog became so famous that the Barron Knights wrote a chart-topping pop song about them, called "Get down Shep!"

There have been 16 presenters on Blue Peter, most of whom have stayed with the programme for a long time. They have gone on to do all kinds of things. Valerie Singleton is now a financial journalist, Peter Purves runs a video company, Christopher Wenner makes documentary films. Sarah is on "Going Live" on Saturday mornings. Lesley Judd is a television presenter, and Janet joined "Open Air". Tina Heath has gone back to acting and looking after Jemma, who was almost born on Blue Peter! Tina was examined by her doctor on the programme when she was pregnant, and with the aid of an amplified stethoscope, viewers were able to hear her baby's heartbeats broadcast live from the womb.

In the year that we celebrate thirty years of Blue Peter we also salute Biddy Baxter, who has been the programme's Editor for twenty six of those years ... Her name appears on the front of this book, though she has not written this article. Presenters and producers and directors have come and gone, but Biddy remained the programme's inspiration and driving force until stepping down in June.

The secret of the success of Blue Peter is that Biddy has never, for a moment, accepted second best for an audience that she believed should be given the best that television could offer.

Janet Ellis created a record with her four mile free fall.

Peter Duncan became Blue Peter's action man in 1980. One of his most hair-raising assignments was washing Big Ben's face!

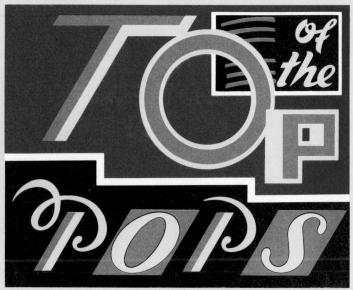

Hi there, pop pickers, it's TOP OF THE POPS, with your special guest DJ, ... it's Mark Curry.

That's how I thought things would go when I suggested we did a film behind-the-scenes with Top of the Pops. The brainboxes who run Blue Peter thought it would be much more interesting if I joined in at the sharp end – as a Floor Assistant. That's the bottom rung of the BBC ladder – the person who's responsible for making sure all the groups turn up on time for their rehearsals in the studio. It's certainly a key job, but not quite like the DJ's!

As soon as I met Nick Wood, the real Floor Assistant assigned to Top of the Pops, I quickly forgot any ideas I had about the job being easy. Nick gave me a set of "cans" – headphones connected to the control room, so I'd be able to hear the "talkback" – all the instructions given by the director. Next we did a tour of dressing rooms. Dressing room 5 was for T'Pau, and Nick asked me if I'd look after them for the day. Like lots of people, I'm a big fan of Carol Decker and the rest of the band, and I'd met Dean Howard on Blue Peter, so I was really pleased I'd be seeing the whole group.

Then rehearsals got started, but where *were* T'Pau?

Chart-toppers T'Pau were my charges for the day. I had to meet them, get them into the studio on time, and most important of all, buy them tea!

Carol Decker, T'Pau's lead singer, has a reputation for looking great. She said she likes to keep the band well-turned out, but she doesn't enjoy ironing as much as the pop papers say!

It takes a whole day and a night to get the Top of the Pops studio ready including bringing in the massive set and organising the complicated lighting rig.

The whole day was a rush! In and out of the studio, with the director's voice constantly in my ear, through the headphones floor assistants wear.

By the time their limousine pulled into BBC Television Centre they were over half an hour late. Their limousine had broken down, they explained as I rushed them towards their dressing room.

T'Pau's rehearsal was at half-past three in the afternoon. This was the "dress run", which not only meant I had to make sure they were in the outfits they'd wear for the recording, but it was also the only time the lighting and all the special effects, like dry ice and smoke, are used before it's done for real. Everything seemed to go very smoothly, so I was told to "release" the band until the evening. It sounds like they were being let out of jail or a zoo, but it's television talk, meaning they weren't needed for a while.

During the afternoon, I did actually get to be Gary Davies for a bit. On Top of the Pops, the Floor Assistants are often asked to stand in for the DJs during the rehearsals. That's because a lot of them are busy doing their radio shows and don't arrive at the studio till the last minute. "Now at Number 9, up six places, it's T'Pau with "Valentine"! Nothing to it really.

It was shortly after that, I heard my name being called by the director up in the control room, or gallery. While I was clambering up the steps, I imagined Paul Ciani the studio director might want to tell me what a brilliant DJ I'd make. But all he wanted to say was that everyone in the gallery was feeling very dry, and could I possibly bring them some fizzy water.

Just before recording time, with the band all made up (everyone has to wear some make-up on television to stop your face looking all shiny), I led them through the maze of the Top of the Pops studio for the last time. They took their positions on stage and another Top of the Pops was underway.

T'Pau's performance was very slick (like all bands on the show, they didn't have to sing and play for real – they mime to a tape they've made before in a recording studio) and the whole show seemed to go well. After so many years of success, it's like a well-oiled machine. Everyone is a part of a team and even if you're a humble Floor Assistant, you do your job efficiently, which helps the programme look so good.

Manuel MENDIVE

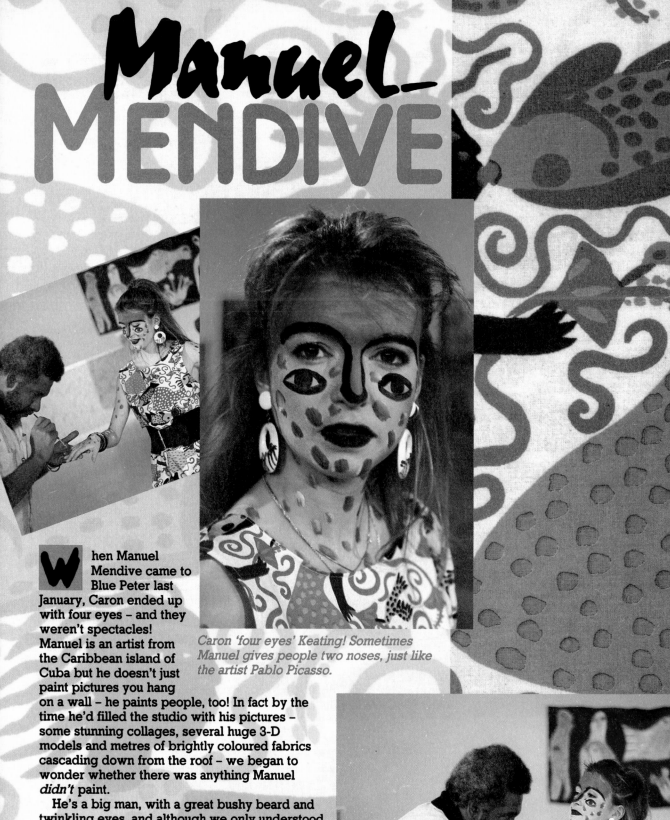

Caron 'four eyes' Keating! Sometimes Manuel gives people two noses, just like the artist Pablo Picasso.

When Manuel Mendive came to Blue Peter last January, Caron ended up with four eyes – and they weren't spectacles! Manuel is an artist from the Caribbean island of Cuba but he doesn't just paint pictures you hang on a wall – he paints people, too! In fact by the time he'd filled the studio with his pictures – some stunning collages, several huge 3-D models and metres of brightly coloured fabrics cascading down from the roof – we began to wonder whether there was anything Manuel *didn't* paint.

He's a big man, with a great bushy beard and twinkling eyes, and although we only understood a few words of Spanish, we soon discovered the ideas Manuel was showing at his first exhibition ever to be held in Britain, were on the themes of water, fish and people. He creates weird shapes and fantasy animals and has had the brilliant idea of transforming his one dimensional pictures into living, breathing art. The results are sensational!

12

He paints his team of five dancers with a brush from head to toe – covering their skin with vivid reds, blues, greens, yellows and purples. There are spots and swirls and squiggles and twirls and extraordinary effects like Caron's second pair of eyes – on her cheeks, below her real eyes. Sometimes he'll even paint an extra nose – sideways on.

One of the dancers had a nose shape that covered the whole of his back and exotic fish appeared swimming up arms and down legs.

Manuel can't be hurried. He spent all day covering human flesh with body paint and it was touch and go whether he'd be finished by the time Blue Peter began. "*Please* ask Manuel if he could hurry up ...", "Tell Manuel there's only five minutes to go ...!!" But it was no use – a true artist can't be ruled by the clock. So it was a great surprise to all of us when our signature tune was played and the dancers sprang into action like exotic tropical birds. We'd never seen them in all their glory before!

Manuel's dancers are famous in Cuba. They recreate Caribbean folk tales and twist and turn into fantasy animals and birds.

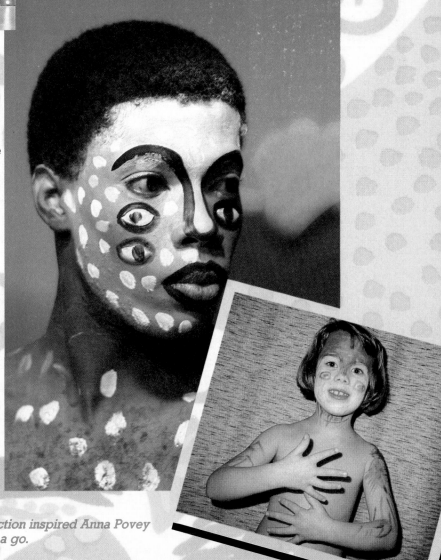

Manuel paints pictures as well as people – and designs collages too.

But when he painted Caron, Manuel *did* work fast. She was wearing a blouse and skirt made from Manuel's specially printed cotton, so her face and arms and legs were painted to match. We dared her to go home before she washed – it would have cheered up the rush hour crowds to have seen a living, breathing painting!

After the programme Anna Povey of Letchworth wrote to us. She'd watched Manuel and had a go at painting *her* body, and her friend Louisa, too. Judging by the results, it won't be long before there's a British artist following in Manuel's footsteps. The only problem is our climate – unlike Cuba where the sun always shines, living paintings in Britain tend to have chattering teeth!

Watching Manuel in action inspired Anna Povey of Letchworth to have a go.

PROFESSOR PEPPER'S GHOST

Do YOU believe in Ghosts? Of course everyone knows they don't really exist – but how DID Mark's head appear without his body? It wasn't a television trick – but a very clever illusion that amazed, mystified and astounded theatre audiences over a hundred years ago!

Professor John Pepper, a Victorian scientist, invented the trick. The actors had a large sheet of glass fitted across the front of the stage. It was angled at forty-five degrees, and the audience could look straight through it and see the background scenery and the leading actors.

A separate area, in the pit below the front of the stage – where the musicians played – was painted black or lined with black felt. If another actor stood there with the spotlight shining on him, the audience would see him reflected by the glass and looking as if he was actually on the stage.

He could appear or vanish as the light was switched on or off which meant hands could appear to pass through bodies and ghostly forms could

appear from nowhere! The Victorians were fond of plays full of evil characters and murders, so Professor Pepper's ghost illusion was extremely useful.

The Professor travelled all over the country, thrilling audiences with his ghost effect – he even took it to Australia in 1879. And as we proved, the trick still works today. No wonder the Victorians believed in ghosts!

15

Yvette Fielding

DATABASE

BORN 23rd September 1968
HOME TOWN Stockport
MIDDLE NAME Paula
STARSIGN
Libra/Virgo (I'm on the cusp)
BROTHERS/SISTERS
One brother, Richard – aged 9
SCHOOL Hillcrest Grammar
FAVOURITE SUBJECTS Art and Drama
HATED SUBJECTS Maths. I was terrible
QUALIFICATIONS
3 O-Levels, 3 O/A Levels, 1 A Level
EARLIEST AMBITION
To be a ballet dancer
FIRST ACTING EXPERIENCE
A Fairy in A Midsummer's Night Dream
HOBBIES WHEN YOUNGER Netball
PETS WHEN YOUNGER Goldfish
FIRST JOB
A cleaner in a hotel at the weekend
FAVOURITE COLOUR Blue
FAVOURITE FOOD Chinese
LEAST FAVOURITE FOOD French
FAVOURITE SPORTS
Horse riding and show jumping
FAVOURITE BAND Inxs
FAVOURITE ALBUM
Riptide by Robert Palmer
FAVOURITE TV SHOW Moonlighting
FAVOURITE STAR Meryl Streep
FAVOURITE CLOTHES I like suits
**FAVOURITE WAY OF SPENDING
SATURDAY** Shopping
**BEST WAY OF SPENDING SPARE
TIME** Sleeping and going for long
walks with Bonnie
BEST FILM EVER Poltergeist
CAR A black Ford Fiesta XR2
**ENJOYED DOING MOST ON BLUE
PETER** Bobsleigh, Showjumping films
**FOUND MOST FRIGHTENING ON
BLUE PETER** Canoeing film and
Ice Hockey
MOST WANT TO DO ON BLUE PETER
Learn to fly an aeroplane
**BEST PART OF BEING ON
BLUE PETER** Doing so many
different things
**WORST PART OF BEING ON BLUE
PETER** Learning lines
BAD HABITS
I don't eat any healthy food
**COUNTRY MOST WANTS TO
VISIT AND WHY**
U.S.A. – because I've heard so
much about it and would like to
see it for myself
PERSON MOST RESPECTS AND WHY
My Grandma – she's just brill!
AMBITION Just to be happy

1. That's me at Blackpool aged five. 2. Fifth Form, Hillcrest Grammar School, Summer 1985. 3. With Aaron Brown alias George, my co-star in "Seaview". 4. My first proper day on Blue Peter with Flat-Foot Clogging Champion, Ira Bernstein. 5. One of the high points of my Blue Peter career so far – jumping at Olympia.

YF

SOUTH STACK ABSEIL

Bird-watching is often a cold and solitary occupation, and, if it's sea-birds you're interested in, it can be quite dangerous, too. But, as millions of enthusiasts will tell you, the moment when you get a rare bird framed in your binoculars is one of the most exciting experiences in the world, and worth every scrap of discomfort you have endured.

South Stack, on Anglesey in Wales, is a steep rocky crag which is one of the best places in Britain for spotting sea-birds. The best time is round about April, when the birds return from a winter at sea for breeding in the spring.

I went there in February – on a bright and frosty morning. The reason for the trip was not to spot birds, but to do a job of work that would make watching sea-birds safe and even comfortable. When the puffins, guillemots and razorbills return from the sea to build their nests, the places they choose are about 20 metres above a whirling torrent of sea, and about 70 metres from the top of a sheer cliff – a place to frighten the life out of the most intrepid bird watcher.

The Royal Society for the Protection of Birds, had an idea for observing the birds in detail, round the clock, in absolute safety. They thought that if you put a remotely controlled television camera down in the nesting area, you would be able to carry out detailed observation of the whole nesting process. A great idea. There was only one snag. How do you get the camera down the cliff?

A dramatic shot of the camera being fixed into position. I'm on the left tightening the final nut.

Peter Holden's to blame! Thanks to him I found myself dangling off the South Stack cliffs.

Going over the top! The sea is seventy metres below!

Inching our way down to the nesting ledge. I'm the blob in the bright red. The Blue Peter cameraman is in the slightly higher group on the right.

You've guessed it!

Peter Holden, our friend from the RSPB had an idea.

"That Irish girl on Blue Peter is always climbing up and down things. Maybe we should give her a call?" Seriously, though, this was a job for the experts, and there were experts near at hand in the shape of the Holyhead Mountain Rescue team.

Terry Porter looked down the sheer wall of the cliff to the boiling sea below. "No real problem there, Caron. It's an abseiling job."

That was what I was afraid of! Last year when I had to switch on the Christmas lights in Bristol, they made me abseil down a 70 metre high building, dressed as Snow White, with the Royal Marines as the seven dwarfs, and that was bad enough. This was an identical assignment – except that it was twice the height, with a raging torrent at the bottom. And there was the small matter of taking a television camera down with us and bolting it to the rock!

"What are *you* going to be doing, Peter?" I asked. "I'll be in charge – up here" he replied.

The descent team consisted of Terry, mountaineers Graham White and David Williams, with Ron Rigby, a television technician, to fit up the television camera, and, of course, John Record our Blue Peter mountaineering cameraman. Every time you see a picture of me in hazardous circumstances, there's got to be a Blue Peter cameraman with me, having an equally hazardous time.

Terry devised a method of getting

the camera down the cliff, by using the same technique as for rescuing an injured climber. Graham and David and I were going to abseil slowly down, manoeuvring a stretcher containing the television camera and all the gear needed to bolt it to the cliff. I always feel scared before I start on an assignment like this, but once I'm in the hands of experts like Graham, Dave and Terry, I somehow take on their professional attitude to the job. Confidence, I'm happy to say, can be just as infectious as fear, and I know which I'd rather catch!

I buckled the familiar straps around my thighs, put on my safety helmet, remembered not to look down, and gently lowered myself over the edge. "Oh, Mark Curry, you should be with us now" I murmured.

Inch by inch we dropped down the sheer rock face, my feet braced against the granite, my body curled round the stretcher. The ceaseless roar of the sea got nearer and nearer. I was slightly comforted by the chucka-chucka of helicopter blades above, which told me that the RAF Rescue Team was keeping an eye on us.

By the time we reached the spot I felt confident enough to wield a spanner to help Ron bolt the camera to the rock. Ron pushed in the plug and threw the switch – and I pushed myself out in front of the lens so that I could make a face at

Peter Holden, watching the monitor in the safety of a snug room at the Nature Centre. It was my first live television appearance dangling from a rope 50 metres from the cliff edge!

I began the slow climb back to the top of the cliff where Peter was waiting to pull me back to feel the firm flat ground beneath my feet again.

I went back into the Nature Centre to see the result of our handiwork with my own eyes. It really was magnificent. The camera could pan and tilt, giving all-round vision, as well as zooming in to give us frame-filling details of the birds.

From now on at South Stack, people will be able to watch the whole nesting process, from mating and egg-laying through to hatching and fledging. It was a breakthrough that would not only teach the ornithologists more about bird behaviour, but would provide many magic moments for enthusiasts like me, without the need to risk their necks at the end of a 60 metre rope!

This is what it was all for – the TV screen in the Visitor Centre. Bird-watchers can get close-up views of guillemots nesting and chicks hatching.

With about 3,000 birds, the guillemot colony at South Stack is one of the biggest in Wales.

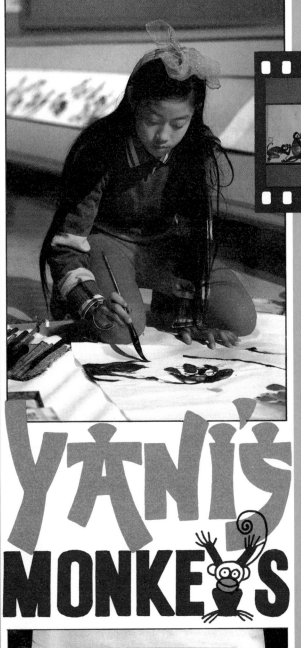

YANI'S MONKEYS

Imagine painting over four thousand pictures ... having exhibitions in countries all over the world ... appearing on TV programmes because you are a famous artist! It sounds like a dream but it's the true life story of a twelve year old girl from China called Yani! When she came on Blue Peter, we filled the studio with Yani's paintings. Most of them were monkeys – there were seventy-seven of them on one picture alone! Here's her remarkable story.

Yani lives with her mother and father in Gongcheng, a town in South China. She began painting when she was two and a half years old. Her father is an artist and one day Yani picked up a piece of charcoal and tried to copy what her Daddy was doing. At first she drew circles. Then she tried to draw her father's face. It was only scribbles, but her parents encouraged her.

Near Yani's house was a park where monkeys swung amongst the trees – like squirrels do in our country. Yani was fascinated by the monkeys. The story goes that once, when she was walking with her father by the banks of a river, Yani began collecting pebbles. "They're monkeys," she said. "Look! This is a monkey's nose and these are his eyes – and these are baby monkeys being hugged by their mothers." After that, Yani's parents gave her a pet monkey, which she called Lida. Yani fed her and looked after her, and then began to paint her famous monkey pictures. There are monkeys climbing, somersaulting, leaping, jumping, riding piggy-back, even picking each other's fleas! The monkeys are often up to tricks and seem to leap off the paper.

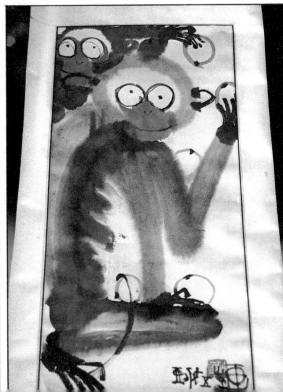

Yani painted this monkey when she was 4 years old.

21

Yani uses brushes and coloured ink and paint and is such a clever artist she can make her paintings come to life with only a few strokes. Once, after a party at her home, some of Yani's uncles drank too much wine. A few days later, she painted three pictures where mischievous monkeys climb up a huge wine bottle, knock it over and drink so much wine they end up flat on the floor. She called the last painting "Dead Drunk!"

The paintings don't need explaining and Yani can't really explain why she creates them! She concentrates so hard, she won't paint and talk at the same time. But when Yani visited the Blue Peter studio she told us – with the help of our interpreter, Yin – she paints monkeys because they are so lively and that she will always want to paint. "How quickly can you create a picture?" I wanted to know. "Six minutes," came the reply! We were so busy talking, neither of us noticed Bonnie – as inquisitive as ever – walking right over the picture Yani had started, sticking her nose in a huge paint tin, and having a long drink! Luckily it *wasn't* as bad as it seemed. Yani had filled the tin with water to mix her paints.
"Could you put Bonnie in your picture?" I asked. "Of course," said Yani.

Yani's monkeys are always up to tricks – like knocking over a huge bottle of wine … and ending up "dead drunk"!

Yani painted a picture especially for Blue Peter – including a portrait of Bonnie!

By the end of the programme, Yani had finished a beautiful painting of grapes cascading down from a vine. At the bottom was a lion – no, it *was* a dog! Bonnie, looking very Chinese with great big bulging eyes. I think Yani had got her own back! But we're very proud to own a painting by one of the most remarkable artists in the world. We'll never forget Yani, or her monkeys!

THE EMPEROR'S WARRIORS

Over two thousand years ago in China, the mighty Emperor Qin Shi Huangdi decreed that when he died an army would stand guard over his grave for all eternity. Hundreds of thousands of people began work, sculpting, casting and moulding the troops in this extraordinary army, for the Emperor's eternal bodyguard was to consist of pottery figures made out of terracotta.

The faithful soldiers stood guard until our own time, when the Emperor's long sleep was finally disturbed, and the greatest archaeological discovery of all time was uncovered. It has been called the Eighth Wonder of the World. It is a unique and awesome memorial to a fearsome ruler, the first man to unify China under one leader.

In the burial chamber were found seven and a half *thousand* infantrymen, plus chariots and charioteers, horses, even a general's command post. Every figure was lifesize and, the features on the faces of the soldiers are so individual, that experts believe the real-life troops in Emperor Qin's army may each have acted as models. The enormous scale of the work involved in creating the burial chamber makes the mind boggle. It's four square miles in area – as big as a medium-sized town like Cambridge. Even now, not all of it has been excavated. And there are stories of such things as poisoned rivers of mercury guarding the innermost sanctum of the Emperor's resting place.

This display of mini terracotta warriors in the studio gives a good idea of the way the warriors were found.

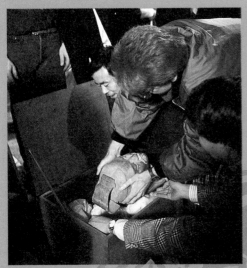
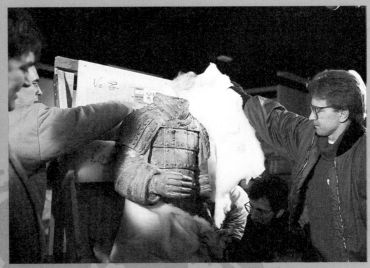

Easy does it! Mark gingerly lifts the head of a warrior from its travelling case. The warrior's body is encased in protective wrapping.

What is on show has become one of China's most famous tourist attractions. But few people in Britain have seen the Terracotta Army face to face. So when we heard that six of the figures, along with other pieces from the burial chamber, were coming to London for an exhibition, we decided we must grab this once-in-a-lifetime chance. We filmed the soldiers for everyone who wouldn't be able to come to London and see them.

The figures arrived carefully swaddled in miles of that bubbly stuff that's fun to pop. Once they were unwrapped, enormous care was taken putting them into position for the exhibition. Mark was allowed to help and was amazed to discover that the standing figures have detachable heads, which simply rest on the shoulders of the soldiers without being fixed at all. He lowered the first head on very gingerly, with a Chinese expert helping – two pairs of hands are safer than one!

Close up you see why the Emperor's Terracotta Army is so important to archaeologists and historians. It's not simply the number of pieces that were found – it's also the incredible detail that went into the making of each one. You can see exactly how their armour was made, down to the rivets in the metal, you can see exactly what weapons they used, and on the kneeling figures you can even see the tread on a shoe. All this provides an exact record of any army dating from the year 220 B.C.

Many of the weapons found in the chambers weren't terracotta copies, but real ones, like the bronze crossbow in the exhibition. This was a frighteningly powerful weapon, used to fire bronze bolts into an enemy before a charge. It's believed that the Chinese crossbow was the most advanced weapon in the world at that time. Although Chinese armies never came into contact with European ones, historians think if they had, they would easily have beaten the legions of Rome or Alexander the Great's Macedonians. Those armies had nothing as good as the crossbow, and their simpler armour and shields would not have stopped the flying bolts.

There are still more secrets to be uncovered from the Qin dynasty. The existence of the Terracotta Army has been known about for a very long time, because its construction

Mark unwraps a reconstruction of a bronze crossbow – the deadliest weapon in the Chinese armoury.

Spot the warrior! One of these dummies is two thousand years old!

Mark comes face to face with a terracotta chariot horse, one of twenty-four found in the tombs.

This must be the most unusual inspection of the troops the Queen's ever done! Her Majesty visited the warriors in their pits in 1986.

was written about in the ancient Chinese histories. But waves of rebels were thought to have destroyed most of it just a few years after the mighty Qin died. So when some people digging a well in 1974 accidentally stumbled on a pit containing six thousand terracotta figures, standing to attention in straight lines, archaeologists were thrilled by the scale of the find and delighted to discover the ancient histories had been wrong – most of the Warriors survived after all.

Further digging revealed another one thousand four hundred warriors, together with ninety chariots. And the Emperor Qin's journey into the afterlife was made with more than just his army. He also took terracotta horses and dogs to go hunting with. The Emperor's many wives were not so lucky however – they too joined their master in his tomb, not as terracotta copies, but as the victims of sacrifice. And the Histories tell of the workers who built the secret passageways and entrances of the tomb being shut up forever inside, so that nobody would live to reveal a way into it.

So far the Chinese have not attempted to penetrate what could well be the greatest jewel in the whole complex at Mount Li the gravesite. They know where the Emperor himself is buried, but at present there are no plans to dig into the man made hill. It's not that the Chinese are frightened about the nasty legends (besides the rivers of mercury, there's one about automatic crossbows set to fire at grave robbers – it's all straight out of Indiana Jones!), more probably

they're just not in any great hurry. After all the Emperor's been there for two thousand years, and the Terracotta Army was only discovered fifteen years ago. Meanwhile, people in the West are itching to find out what's in the Emperor's tomb and can't wait for the Chinese to dig it up!

The London Exhibition of the Emperor's Terracotta Warriors was a great success – tens of thousands visited it in the two months it was on. It was also a big hit with Blue Peter viewers. Not only were we able to bring two life-size replica warriors to the studio, we launched a competition with mini terracotta warriors as prizes.

The response was the biggest the programme's ever had in its entire thirty year history – over a quarter of a million entries. What other proof is needed that the legends and achievements of the Emperor Qin Shi Huangdi still stir the imagination two thousand, one hundred and ninety-eight years after his death?

HEAD Gardener

The saddest announcement we had to make this year was the death of our dear friend Percy Thrower – "Britain's Head Gardener". Percy had worked with Blue Peter for fourteen years. He'd made 200 broadcasts from the garden he designed for us and even now, we almost expect to see him when we're out there. Digging the vegetable plot, pruning the roses, or planting one of those marvellous splashes of colour in the Italian Sunken Garden beds.

Percy helped us start the Blue Peter garden in 1974 – the veg we grow supply our Old People's Centre in Deptford. The Italian Sunken Garden was built in 1978, and saplings from our tree nursery were sent to places hit by the hurricane of 1987.

Why were we so fond of him? He was certainly a very hard task master – there was no skiving around with Percy in charge, and no sheltering in the greenhouse when it rained, either. Snow or shine, Percy got stuck in – and he expected Blue Peter presenters to get stuck in, too! Strangely enough, we all loved him for being so firm and tough. You always knew where you were with Percy – and the great thing was, you learned so much from him.

Successions of Blue Peter presenters who started off without the slightest interest in gardening became wildly enthusiastic when seeds they'd

Giant Sunflowers! Percy gave Janet Ellis and Simon Groom some good growing tips, but their flowers were beaten by Blue Peter viewers!

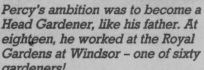

Percy aged eleven, in 1924. His pets included a tame magpie, a cat and a jackal, as well as these pigeons.

Once Percy saw the Queen, with Princess Elizabeth and Princess Margaret, but he wasn't allowed to speak to them.

Percy's ambition was to become a Head Gardener, like his father. At eighteen, he worked at the Royal Gardens at Windsor – one of sixty gardeners!

Percy's radio programme for children "Our Garden", began in 1950 – it was very popular.

Top comedians Morcambe and Wise invited Percy to take part in their Show.

planted under Percy's expert eye actually grew! There's nothing like the taste of home-grown veg. Carrots, peas, runner beans, beetroot, Jerusalem artichokes, radish, lettuce, tomatoes, cucumbers and loads of herbs were all produced from one tiny plot at the back of the BBC's canteen measuring 4 by 3.5 metres, and our small unheated greenhouse.

There were exotic vegetables, too, like kohl rabi and sea kale beet and a whole rainbow of flowers – from the tulips, daffodils, hyacinths and primulas in the Spring to the roses, sweetpeas and Percy's favourites, the fuchsias, in the summer. Not

forgetting our attempts to grow Giant Sunflowers – although we were always beaten by Blue Peter viewers!

Percy left school at fourteen to become a humble gardener's boy on a large estate in Buckinghamshire and eventually became Britain's most famous gardener. But he was never big-headed and never too grand to give advice to anyone who asked for his help. Often in the Blue Peter garden, we'd be working out a complicated sequence for the cameras when a passer-by would button-hole Percy. "My broadbeans look sick – how can I get rid of blackfly?" And Percy would tell them what to do, without a hint that he was too busy to bother.

It was typical of Percy that he carried on working almost to the end of his life.

He'd had a serious heart operation and made a good recovery, when he had to return to hospital with problems with his legs that prevented him from walking. He'd already told us he'd have to

In 1976 Madame Tussaud's made this waxwork of Percy.

retire from the Blue Peter garden and on Friday March 11th Mark went to Percy's ward in Wolverhampton's Royal Hospital with Blue Peter film cameras, to show viewers how Percy was getting on. The big surprise was our present – a video cassette of Percy's life with highlights like his wedding to Connie in 1939, his first radio broadcast from Shrewsbury in 1947, his first gardening programme for children in 1950, and broadcasts like his appearance on the Morcambe and Wise Show and This Is Your Life.

Chris Crowder became the new Blue Peter gardener on March 14th 1988.

The nurses let Mark play it to Percy and at the end, he presented him with the programme's highest award – a Gold Blue Peter Badge! That was an even greater surprise than the video. Percy was thrilled to bits. He said it was as big an honour as his Victoria Medal of Honour of the Royal Horticultural Society and his M.B.E.

We asked Percy's advice about our new gardener, and he recommended a young man Yvette had met, when she filmed the famous Topiary Gardens at Cumbria's Levens Hall. His name was Chris Crowder and he was already following in Percy's footsteps. Chris also went into gardening straight from school, and at 23, he'd been made Head Gardener. "He's alright, that lad", Percy had said. "He knows what he's doing and he'll keep you in order!" How well Percy knew the problems of licking Blue Peter presenters into shape!

Chris admired Percy and planned to visit him at Easter. But it was not to be. Just seven days after we filmed Percy in hospital, he died – aged 75. The letters from Blue Peter viewers were incredible. We knew Percy was popular and the letters proved just how much children and people of all ages had loved him. Time after time they said "*Please* have a memorial to Percy in the Blue Peter Garden". There were suggestions for fuchsias, for roses, for trees – including a Magnolia – the name of Percy's house. And in the end, we decided to plant two bushes of the beautiful pink rose, named in his honour and two of his favourite plants – fuchsias – the hardy variety that should flower all through the Summer. The flower bed is also planted with forget-me-nots and polyanthus and the plaque is very simple. It says:

IN MEMORY OF
PERCY THROWER
1913 – 1988

Rags TO RICHES

"Walk on …"

"Steady …"

"Keep your head up … that's right!"

The first thing that strikes you when you see a class of disabled riders is what a vast scene the word "disabled" covers. The blind, the deaf, the disabled in the mind and the disabled in the body. Some lived a perfectly normal life until a car crash. Some have been disabled since birth.

"Now give your horse at pat to say thank you for the ride. Good. Now show me how you get off your horse … Very good".

The rider was Louise who suffers from Spina Bifida. The helper was Her Royal Highness The Princess Royal, who is also the President of the Riding for the Disabled Association.

The place: the indoor riding school at Buckingham Palace Mews.

The Princess Royal is President of the RDA. Even people with the severest disabilities have learned to ride, thanks to the Association's 635 Groups. Princess Anne maintained how important the helpers are. They need special training – as well as the horses. In 1975 Blue Peter viewers provided the programme's first pony, Rags. She was also trained by Tessa Martin Bird and Princess Anne was the first to ride her off the lunge rein. ▼

◄ *Louise has Spina Bifida. Being able to ride gives her the chance to be like other children.*

Yvette knows exactly what being able to ride means to Barnaby. She was an RDA helper before she joined Blue Peter.

The occasion: the launch of the twenty-fifth Blue Peter Appeal.

It is our second Appeal for Riding for the Disabled. In 1975 Blue Peter viewers provided Rags the first Blue Peter pony, who in her time gave more than ten thousand rides to disabled children. When Rags died in March 1986, seven year old Zoe Price wrote to Blue Peter.

"I'm sorry Rags is dead. I hope you get a replacement for her". And Sarah Dines from Lynn in Cheshire said: "In memory of Rags would it be possible for Blue Peter viewers to buy another horse so that many more disabled children can discover the wonderful sense of freedom that riding can give?"

One in every ten of all the children in the world is disabled. Think of that. How many are there

Our Depot at Bradford received more than double our Target of parcels of old wool and cotton.

in your class? Thirty? If that's so and your class represented the whole world, three of your class mates would have some kind of disability. Of course, everyone feels sorry for someone who can't walk properly, but have you ever stopped to think what it's really like? Not being able to go down a lovely rugged path, because it would be too bumpy for a wheelchair, or too difficult in calipers, and to be forever in a sitting position unable to see over the heads of the people around you. And perhaps worst of all, always being on the touch line whilst other people are joining in the game. Being able to get on a horse could change all that. Doing something active with friends … going places where wheel

The scene at St Mary's Church Hall, where the people of Haddington collected 18 huge parcels of rags.

The RDA group from Shelf, near Bradford, delivered their rags direct to the Depot.

chairs can never go. Looking down on the world instead of always looking up. Yvette, who had been an RDA voluntary helper before she joined Blue Peter, said:

"In my experience there's no doubt what it means to someone like Louise who's permanently handicapped, to be able to sit on a horse and move about freely. She'd never be able to do that on her own".

And The Princess Royal told viewers, "For many disabled children, riding is the highlight of their lives. And there are many more children we would like to give that opportunity to."

These were the hard facts that you, the viewers had to face. We needed one thousand tonnes of rags or, put it another way, forty million hankies. With that we would be able to provide Rags' replacement, fully trained, and vital equipment for each one of the 635 RDA Groups in Great Britain. Mounting blocks, saddles with special supports, sheepskin covers for riders needing soft support, hard hats and ladder reins for those who cannot use their hands.

In twenty-five years Blue Peter viewers have never let us down. And 1987 was no exception. Rags came pouring in from all over the country and because of delivery help from Lynx and the Post Office's fantastic offer of FREEPOST, our Bradford Depot was busy right from the start. There were unusual donations like a load of old

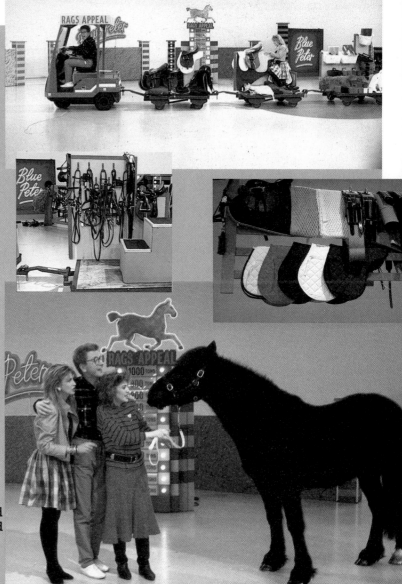

We've Got It! On January 11th 1988 we reached our Rags Appeal Target and our new pony made his first TV appearance.

curtains from a School hall in Maidstone; sad ones, like the clothes no longer wanted because their owners had died; even the canopy from an enormous four-poster bed. And once again, viewers of the British Forces Broadcasting Services in Germany and Cyprus held collections and arranged for *their* rags to be flown to Britain!

There were one or two anxious moments when we wondered if this was going to be the first year we didn't make it. But on Monday 11th January 1988, a clatter of tiny hooves rang out on the studio floor.

YOU HAD DONE IT AGAIN!

The hooves belonged to a great character who Blue Peter viewers were going to call Jet on account of the fact that, apart from a white

Your old wool and cotton also provides equipment for all the RDA's 635 Groups. Jet's trainer, Tessa Martin-Bird, brought some of it to the studio.

Blue Peter viewers chose "Jet" as our pony's name. Here he is training on the lunge reign with Tessa and becoming familiar with the weight of a rider on his back.

blaze on the front of his head, he is inky black all over. Jet is a Dales pony, chosen because this breed is tough and sturdy yet has the perfect docile, friendly temperament needed for an RDA pony.

He demonstrated his amiable temperament by biting Yvette's finger in his first minute in the Blue Peter studio! We decided that showed he had spirit and wasn't "just a plug" as The Princess Royal would have said. Later on, when Jet was put through his paces by our old friend Tessa Martin Bird, who also trained Rags, there was no doubt that we had a character on our hands for the next year.

A lot of your mothers and fathers, aunts and uncles would have contributed to the very first Blue Peter Appeal. It makes us very proud to think that when it comes to doing something extra to help someone who is worse off than you are, after twenty-five years Blue Peter viewers can still show the way!

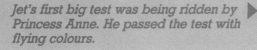

"He's certainly an individual and he doesn't seem to be afraid of anything," was Tessa's first assessment.

Not only did you provide Jet, but the studio was filled to overflowing with equipment for every one of those 635 RDA Groups. The final total was two thousand three hundred and eight tonnes of rags – over double the amount we had asked for.

Jet's first big test was being ridden by Princess Anne. He passed the test with flying colours. ▶

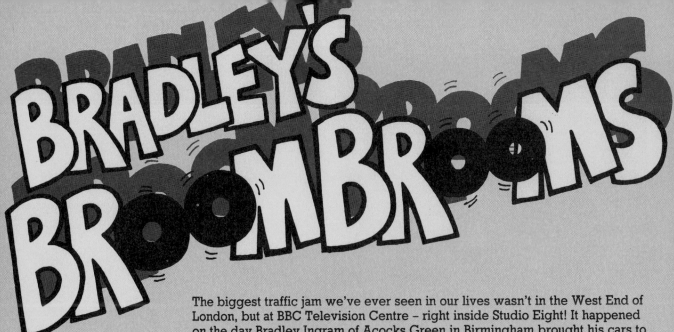

BRADLEY'S BROOMBROOMS

The biggest traffic jam we've ever seen in our lives wasn't in the West End of London, but at BBC Television Centre – right inside Studio Eight! It happened on the day Bradley Ingram of Acocks Green in Birmingham brought his cars to Blue Peter – all ten thousand of them!

They were *model* cars, of course. Bradley started collecting them and simply forgot to stop. The remarkable thing was that he's not an old man who's devoted a lifetime to his hobby, carefully scouring junkshops and jumble sales for models to add to his precious collection. Bradley collected the whole lot in just four years. He began when he was ten and he brought the mega-jam to the studio when he was fourteen.

He had them all – Dinky, Matchbox, Corgi – piled up on top of each other, crammed into boxes, vintage cars and sleek modern racers, old buses, lorries and trams, bulldozers and tipper trucks, fire engines, ambulances and taxis by the dozen, even Chitty Chitty Bang Bang and Basil Brush models. When we'd finally laid them all out on display for the programme (which took hours!), we had not only the biggest traffic jam ever, but one of the most impressive collections we've ever seen in the studio.

Just some of Bradley Ingram's ten thousand models!

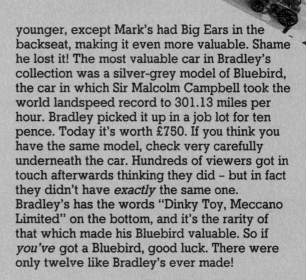

Bradley's models include modern buses, and coaches, as well as ancient horse-drawn wagons.

Some of the most unusual and valuable models feature characters like Noddy and Basil Brush. Behind Basil is the rarest model of all – Malcolm Campbell's Bluebird.

The really nice thing about Bradley though, is that he wasn't totally bonkers about his collection. The models were a great hobby which he enjoyed for four years, but the reason the whole lot appeared on Blue Peter was because Bradley was planning to *sell* them. His family was moving to a new, smaller house and his Mum had finally put her foot down. "Those cars have got to go, Bradley." She must have been totally fed up getting a faceful of Dinkies every time she opened a bedroom door.

Bradley must have spent every penny of his pocket money and whatever he's earned over the last four years buying his cars. But it was certainly well worth it. He showed us several models worth forty or fifty pounds each. His Noddy car was like one Mark had when he was younger, except Mark's had Big Ears in the backseat, making it even more valuable. Shame he lost it! The most valuable car in Bradley's collection was a silver-grey model of Bluebird, the car in which Sir Malcolm Campbell took the world landspeed record to 301.13 miles per hour. Bradley picked it up in a job lot for ten pence. Today it's worth £750. If you think you have the same model, check very carefully underneath the car. Hundreds of viewers got in touch afterwards thinking they did – but in fact they didn't have *exactly* the same one. Bradley's has the words "Dinky Toy, Meccano Limited" on the bottom, and it's the rarity of that which made his Bluebird valuable. So if *you've* got a Bluebird, good luck. There were only twelve like Bradley's ever made!

A boxed set of vintage cars (left) is one more of Bradley's highlights.

Personal ORGANISERS

There's no need to spend a fortune on the latest craze to help busy people! The Blue Peter Personal Organiser is mostly made from bits and pieces you'll find lying around at home. And once you've made the cover, you can fill up your Organiser any way you like.

The great thing about these personal organisers is that you can design one yourself so there won't be another like it anywhere in the world!

You can chose your favourite colour or pattern for the cover and for the files inside, you can use spare sheets of graph paper from an exercise book, you can make a diary by cutting up a calendar and plastic pockets for keeping your bus pass or library ticket safe can be made from old transparent plastic files. If you don't have any files you can make them from freezer bags of the cellophane from a box of chocolates. There's a useful pocket at the front, a place to stick a notepad – and at the back, a pocket for a train or bus timetable.

YOU WILL NEED:
Stiff card (eg a porridge packet).
Sticky-backed plastic.
2 binding rings – available from most stationers.
A length of ribbon.
Self-sticking tape fastener.
Coloured card.
Assorted paper.
Glue or double-sided sticky tape.

1
Decide on the size of the paper you want inside. Paper for Personal Organisers is usually twice as high as it is wide. For a really cheap way of buying paper, get hold of a pad that already has 4 holes punched down the side so that if you divide the paper into four and cut it out you will have enough paper for the next year or two!

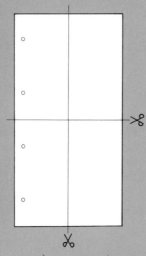

2
The cover is made from any old stiff piece of card. Take a piece of your paper and put it on the cardboard. Mark out the size of your Organiser, making the cover a bit bigger than the paper.

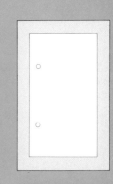

3
You'll need 3 bits of card altogether, two pieces the same size for the front and back and also a piece for the spine or centre of the Organiser, just over the width of a ruler. Lay them side by side with the spine in the middle and cut out a piece of sticky backed plastic, a few centimetres *bigger* then the cardboard and stick the cardboard to the sticky-backed plastic. Make sure that when you stick the spine down, you don't leave a gap. For a neat finish, cut across the corners of the plastic *before* you stick it down on the inside.

STICKY BACKED PLASTIC
CARD   CARD
CARD
STICKY BACKED PLASTIC

4 Once the sticky-backed plastic is on, test the Organiser to make sure it closes properly and then carefully cover the inside with the same sticky-backed plastic cut to the right size.

4 ▼

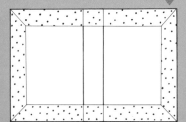

5 The thing that makes these Organisers special is the binding rings which open and close, so that you can add or take away any files from your Organiser any time you like. You can get these rings at a stationers. To fix them in the cover, first mark the position where they are going to go, by taking a piece of your paper and placing it with the holes dead centre on the spine. Then mark the positions of the holes with a pencil.

5 ▶

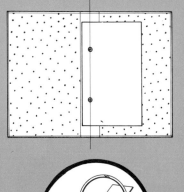

6 Take a small strip of the sticky-backed plastic, push it through the ring, covering the hinge, and stick it down on the spine with the ring on the pencil mark.

Do the same with the other ring. For extra strength, measure the distance from the bottom to the ring and cut some strips of cardboard that size.

6 ▶

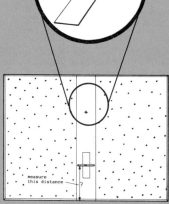

measure this distance

7 Sandwich the pieces together with glue to make a 'block' of card and check that it fits in position. Cover the block with sticky-backed plastic. Make 2 more blocks for the middle and top sections.

Stick them down on to the spine, making sure they are tight up against the rings, preventing them from moving.

7 ▼

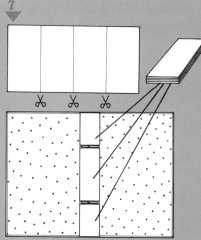

8 To finish the cover, add pockets by cutting two pieces of card, one the width of the cover, the other the height of the cover. Cover them with sticky-backed plastic; Use glue or double-sided sticky tape along three sides to stick them in place inside the cover. These make very useful pockets for timetables, calendars or last minute notes.

8 ▼

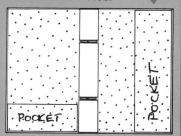

POCKET   POCKET

9 The fastener, is a length of ribbon stuck to the outside of the cover. Leave an over-lapping length of the ribbon on the back cover. Stick on a strip of self-sticking material. Stick the other half of the self-sticking tape to the opening side of the front cover. This makes the Organiser secure, but still gives you instant access when you need it.

10 What goes into your Organiser is totally up to you. To make the different sections easy to find make some dividers by cutting coloured card slightly bigger than the paper, leaving a tag on each one so that when they are in the Organiser, each tag will show above the next.

10 ▶

NOTES

EXPEDITION TO THE
S☭VIET UNION

Watch out Moscow, here comes Yvette! Ms Fielding tries to blend in with the surroundings, outside the Foreign Ministry. ▼

The Soviet Union – the largest country on earth. What things spring into your mind when you hear that name? Snow, ice and fur hats? Unsmiling, grey people who hate foreigners? Missiles on lorries trundling through Moscow, talk of 'bad news' and 'crisis' on the television? When we heard that our request to film inside the Soviet Union had been granted, we didn't know what to expect. All those sad, bad things, for sure, but *surely* there had to be another side to such a huge country. We hoped our five weeks filming would give us a few answers. We weren't disappointed.

Mark catches up with the news, behind a copy of Pravda. You should be able to work out five letters of the Russian alphabet! ▶

38

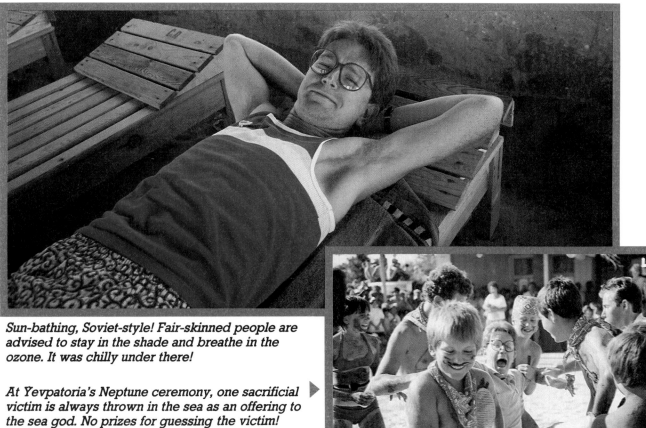

Sun-bathing, Soviet-style! Fair-skinned people are advised to stay in the shade and breathe in the ozone. It was chilly under there!

At Yevpatoria's Neptune ceremony, one sacrificial victim is always thrown in the sea as an offering to the sea god. No prizes for guessing the victim! ▶

We spent our first few days getting to know the capital city, Moscow. It's an absolutely enormous place, at least as big as London, with little cars rushing around the street, weaving in and out of buses and tour coaches. We hadn't expected Moscow to have traffic jams (don't know why we didn't) but they have real beauties, and whenever we needed to be somewhere in a hurry, we were stuck in one. The underground train system was more reliable. All the station names are written in Russian, of course, so unless you read the language, or you knew what the name of your destination looked like, it was all too easy to get lost.

Caron and Yvette were off on their favourite hobby almost as soon as they arrived ... shopping. As it happens, shopping is a very good way to find out about a country, and it tells you an enormous amount about life in the Soviet Union. Compared to Britain, it's very hard to get things, whether it's food, or clothes, or electrical goods. Just think what shopping would be like in Britain, if you couldn't buy things that had come from abroad ... bananas from the West Indies, oranges from Israel, jeans from America, tape recorders and videos from Japan. The Soviet Union doesn't trade much with foreign countries. Most of the things people buy have to be made there, and some things are in very short supply, or aren't made to a very high quality, or don't get made at all.

There was a lot of freedom down at the children's seaside resort of Yevpatoria. It basks

Let your fingers do the walking! Caron has those aches and pains soothed away, to be replaced by bruises! ▶

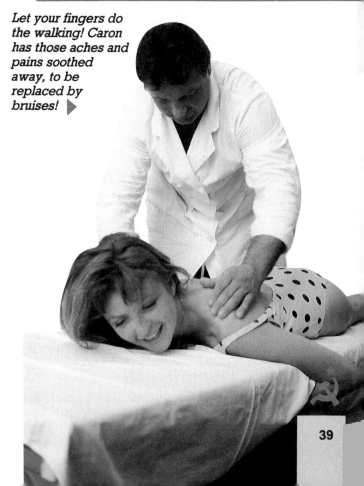

on the sunny Black Sea and while the guests swelter there, they also can choose from a whole range of special treatments that are provided – all included in the price – to make them feel fitter and healthier. Mark discovered that being daubed from head to toe in slimy, smelly mud is considered a luxury, while Caron found out that having a relaxing massage *is* a luxury. Yvette was buried in hot sand – that's supposed to be good for the circulation – and also tried out a frisky spa bath.

Fashion, as girls like Caron and Yvette know it, just doesn't exist in Russia. Everywhere they went, heads were turned and people quite unashamedly stared at their outfits. We filmed in a top clothes store, and thought everything was about fifteen years out of date. But outside, *hundreds* of women were queueing to get in to snap up whatever was on offer. Apparently, it's not that often the shops have new deliveries of anything. 'Trading', as it's called, is very big there, although it's strictly against the rules. People approach you in the street and offer to swap things for your jeans or trainers.

It was a similar story in the supermarkets – empty shelves, with only a few staple foods like bread and rice easily obtainable. And for some reason, absolutely masses of sardines – shelf after shelf of them. We were taken to Moscow's newest supermarket for filming, half-an-hour from the centre on a new housing estate. The shelves there were a bit more full but while we were filming there was a sudden burst of activity, and cartloads of meat, cheese, biscuits and fish started coming out. Word must have quickly gone round the estate, because the place soon filled up, and customers were soon carrying stuffed shopping bags away.

Our adventures with the Moscow Builders at the State Circus. Getting ready, walking into the ring, the spectacular performance, the friendship and support of the Builders – especially Big Yuri – all moments we'll never forget.

40

For us, food was a major problem. When you come from a country like ours, where you can find half a dozen fast food or takeaway restaurants on every high street, where a menu is an indication of what's on offer and not just what the cook would *like* to be able to offer, it is almost impossible to imagine what eating in Moscow is like. Most holidaymakers go there in organised groups, and the hotels feed them.

We were not an organised group. The biggest problem we had each day was not trying to make our films, which is a complicated enough business, but worrying about where we would eat lunch and dinner. Just getting a booking at a restaurant is extremely difficult. And once you get it, you wait hours for your meal and the food isn't very good most of the time. Yvette ate just ice-cream for the first ten days.

At Moscow's wonderful weekly Pet Market, we made friends with Sasha whose kittens looked just like Willow!

In our first week, we went to see one of Moscow's top attractions, the State Circus. It was a great show, with acrobats, trapeze artists, clowns, jugglers and magicians. There were one or two animal acts we weren't so happy about, but it seems the Russian idea of what's acceptable with animals is very different to our own. Through a great stroke of luck, Caron and Yvette were invited to train with the most original act of all – the Moscow Builders. They do an extremely unusual acrobatic act using very long poles, with acrobats suspended from them. It looked breath-taking and very difficult to learn. We had one day!

The Moscow Builders were a great bunch of people. They immediately accepted us and showed us how they practice their routine. It involved being hoisted twenty metres up into the air, hanging on to the arms of an acrobat. After the rehearsal, we were told "you're in"!

Yvette having her portrait painted by a pavement artist. 1987 was the first year artists could work and keep their earnings.

The day of the performance in which we took part, is one to cherish for a long time. We had a quick extra rehearsal, and then went off to get changed. The audience were not to be told that we were two novices from Britain, until *after* we had performed.

So we were extremely nervous, knowing that only a proper and professional performance would do. It went like a dream!

There we were, centre-stage at the Moscow State Circus for the one and only time in our lives, with the audience clapping and cheering as the ringmaster announced our names. Since he was speaking Russian, that was all we could make out, along with the initials "B.B.C."

Those three magic

Bargaining for fruit at Moscow's main private market. The fruitseller has travelled hundreds of miles and fresh fruit is so rare in Moscow, he can charge high prices.

Inside GUM, the giant arcade of shops in the centre of Moscow. It's a must for tourists – just the place to pick up a fur hat (fake, of course!) for about £12. ▼

letters certainly opened a few doors and gave us lots of smiles and hellos. People always came up to us when we were filming and most were very interested when we told

Meeting children at a Kindergarten in Samarkand. The girls are wearing the national costume of the local people, the Uzbeks.

them we were from the BBC. That was especially true once we left Moscow, and started travelling around. People often talk about "Russia" without realising that Russia is only one (although easily the largest) of fifteen republics that make up the Soviet Union. The Russians themselves are just one people in an Empire of almost a hundred different peoples. When we travelled to Vilnius, the capital of Lithuania, the people spoke Lithuanian and the signs were written in the local language first, and Russian second.

Over a thousand miles from Moscow, in Uzbekistan, we saw that really the people had very little in common with Moscow. They looked different, ate different foods, spoke their own language and seemed to live lives of much greater freedom than the fairly restricted feeling we found in Moscow.

Samarkand, the ancient city we

Red Square at sunset. Mark posing in front of the Kremlin Wall.

visited in Uzbekistan, was one of our favourite places. We ate masses of melons, the girls bought lengths of silk and cotton, we all admired the intricate workmanship of the blue-gold mosques, mausoleums and shrines which adorn the city. It was a great shock to arrive back in a wet, cold Moscow at two in the morning after a four hour flight from Samarkand.

It's the ordinary things that show the differences in life between Britain and the Soviet Union. For instance, there are hardly any telephone books over there, and the ones they do have are hopelessly out of date or impossible to get hold of. We did not see one during our entire stay. Unless you know the number you want, telephoning someone is virtually impossible. Not giving people access to telephone numbers is a way of controlling things. It helps the Soviet government stop the spread of information – perhaps it's a difference between a country that is free and one that is not free.

But the Soviet *people* made us welcome, asked us questions, admired our clothes and generally were very friendly and flattered that we were interested in them and their country. We have dozens of delightful memories – of the people we met worshipping at Zagorsk, the big monastery north of Moscow, of the circus performers, of the brilliant young gymnasts we met, of the children on holiday at Artek, the Young Pioneer Camp, of the many guides that helped us in each of the cities we visited.

And as the pictures show, we enjoyed ourselves tremendously. We set out to show viewers sides of the Soviet Union they don't normally see, and we would jump at the chance of returning to the largest country on earth.

Yvette attempts the isometric bars at a top gymnastic school. ▼

Caron in front of her favourite building in Russia: St Basil's Cathedral in Red Square. ▼

43

TOP C

An otherwise normal Saturday in December, but to the frantic Christmas shoppers it must seem that every bus and taxi, car and train in West London has been taken over by CATS! Short-hair, long-hair, pedigree and pet, Siamese and Balinese – they're all heading for the most important date in the cat calendar. It's the day of the National Cat Club Championship Show, held every year at Olympia. And this is a special show in a very special year – the National Cat Club's Centenary.

All the top cat breeders are there, but it's also a day for the ordinary cat lover, who can enter their own moggies in one of the Household Pet Sections for cats without pedigrees. The most famous of the pet sections are the Blue Peter Classes!

Edith Menezes is Blue Peter's Kitty Queen! She's looked after all our cats, including Willow, and helps Caron whittle the entries in the Blue Peter Classes down to a final eight. Edith's also a member of the Governing Council of the National Cat Club, who organise the Show and to celebrate its Centenary, all the Council wore Victorian costume.

It's a busy day for Caron! Not only does she judge the Blue Peter Classes, but she also helps out at the Blue Peter Stand where she meets many viewers and signs lots of autographs.

All the cats have a special grooming before the Show – they have to look their best for the Judges.

CATS

Willow makes a special guest appearance on the Blue Peter Stand

The eight winning cats and owners from the Blue Peter Classes appear on the next programme, when the Supreme Champion is chosen. It's entirely your choice, not even the Editor of Blue Peter gets a vote!

The vote was unanimous. This year's Blue Peter Supreme Champion and winner of the magnificent silver cup was Gobolino, a five year old black cat owned by eight year old Anna Symonds of Letty Green in Hertfordshire.

If you think your cat is a potential Supreme Champion, why don't you enter for the next National Cat Club Show? You can get details of the Blue Peter Classes by sending a stamped addressed envelope to:-

Mrs Betty Walde
11 Pembroke Road
Pound Hill Crawley
Sussex RH10 3TL

Good luck!

Heroine of the Seas

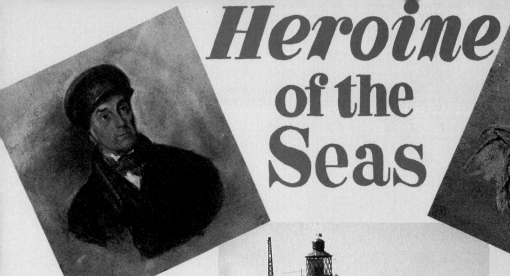

The Lighthouse on Longstone Island warned passing ships of the dangers of the submerged small rocks and islands that make up the Farne Islands.

Grace Darling (above) and her father William. Together they made one of the bravest of all rescues.

The sea storms and rages all around the British Isles. Many ships and many lives have been in peril on the sea and sometimes this danger has inspired tremendous acts of heroism.

Exactly one hundred and fifty years ago, the name of a twenty-two year old heroine was on everyone's lips. Her name was Grace Darling.

Her father, William Darling, was a lighthouse keeper on the Farne Islands off the Northumberland coast. In 1826 he became the first keeper of the new Longstone lighthouse, where the rocks lying close to the surface of the angry sea, had been a hazard to shipping for centuries.

It was in this remote, desolate place that William Darling and his wife Thomasin brought up their seven children. One by one, Grace's brothers and sisters left home. But she stayed on with her elderly parents.

It was a hard, uncomfortable life. Grace cooked the family meals and did the washing in a kitchen that could be flooded with water in heavy seas. She swept and scrubbed the hundred steps leading up to the light itself.

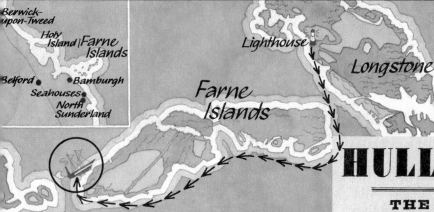

The Longstone Island is seven miles off the Northumberland Coast. Grace lived there alone with her elderly parents, after her six brothers and sisters left home.

The Forfarshire was a steam ship. On 5th September 1838 it set out from Hull, bound for Dundee with sixty-three passengers and crew – only to be wrecked in a tempestuous storm.

After Grace spotted the wreck, she helped her father row their heavy coble through the dangerous seas.

These drawings of the heroic rescue appeared in newspapers and magazines.

The light ruled their lives. It shone from the top of the tower, so that ships could steer by it and keep clear of the deadly rocks. The light had to be kept burning all the hours of darkness, and all the parts had to be kept brightly polished. That light still shines and, in spite of automation, Grace would still recognise some of the machinery today.

September 6th 1838, was a night of fierce autumn storms. Grace helped her father secure the doors and windows. Together they dragged their heavy rowing boat, called a coble, up into shelter and made it fast. Then she went to her bedroom, a little round room below the light.

Out at sea, a ship – the Forfarshire – struggled in the storm. She was a steamship with huge paddle wheels and she was bound from Hull for Dundee, with sixty three passengers and crew. But a boiler leak stopped the engines and the ship had drifted helplessly towards the rocks. Next morning Grace woke and dressed early. In the half light, she saw a dim shape on Big Harcar rocks. She called her father, and they looked through the telescope. A ship was wrecked – it was the Forfarshire!

Then Grace saw movement – a handful of survivors had clambered from the wreck, on to the rocks. They were safe so far, but they were in deadly danger from the next high tide. Grace and her father gazed at them in horror. How could they rescue these people with only their heavy rowing boat, which needed three men to hold her in rough weather?

At the Grace Darling Museum, you can see the actual boat Grace rowed.

When Grace became a national heroine, thousands of souvenirs of the rescue were produced – like this china figure.

Grace could row as strongly as a man. "I will go with you," she said. "Some of the survivors can help us row back!"

Their first task was to drag the coble hundreds of yards across the island, and launch it, with waves breaking over them. To get what shelter they could from the gale, they rowed the long way round the island.

Slowly they moved towards the rocks. The huddled survivors watched breathless until the boat, their only hope of rescue, drew alongside.

As William Darling sprang ashore, Grace held the heavy, clumsy coble steady in the swirling foam and blinding spray, which seemed to force her back against the rocks that had wrecked the Forfarshire. *All* their lives – the survivors, her father's and her own – depended on Grace now.

She held firm, and at last the boat was loaded, and they began the return voyage. Two of the survivors helped to row, and then returned with William to fetch the last of the survivors. By nine o'clock, everyone was back safe and sound in the lighthouse.

For William and Grace, it had all been part of their ordinary work, and Grace only wanted to return to everyday life again. *It was impossible.*

The story of the rescue was told everywhere. Grace was the first newspaper heroine, and soon the whole nation had heard of her. Her portrait was painted, she was invited to take part in a circus and to appear on stage. She was loaded with presents; tourists came to stare at her; there were countless Grace Darling souvenirs and even a popular song was written about her.

Grace hated it. Sadly, she became ill, and died on October 20th 1842, little more than four years after the heroic deed that made her famous and ruined her life. She was only twenty-six years old.

She was buried in Bamburgh churchyard. and they gave her a fine monument, high up on the sea coast, so that passing ships could see it, and remember the heroism of those who struggle to save the lives of those in peril on the sea.

And to commemorate the 150th anniversary of Grace's brave rescue, the RNLI is launching an Appeal. The target is a new lifeboat for North Sunderland. If it is successful, the boat will be called *The Grace Darling.*

Grace's fine monument can be seen by sailors on passing ships.

The RNLI has launched the Grace Darling Appeal to celebrate the 150th anniversary of Grace's rescue.

MAPLINS
TRUE OR FALSE?

Hi-de-Hi!

Hi-de-Hi! Can you spot the real Peggy and Ted? If you turn this page upside down, you'll find the answer!

If you've ever taken part in a play, you'll know one of the worst headaches is finding costumes for all the actors.

So imagine what it's like at the BBC, putting on hundreds of plays and shows each year with casts of thousands! There's no time to make the clothes. Some of them are hired from theatrical costumiers, but in a giant warehouse close to Television Centre, there's a store of a hundred thousand different outfits that all belongg to the BBC.

When Mark and Yvette explored, they found Rowan Atkinson's doublet and hose from Black Adder, space suits from Dr Who, Lenny Henry's trousers, frilly frocks from 'Allo 'Allo, even outfits for chickens, bears, tigers, crocodiles and dancing Spring onions and cucumbers!

But top favourite were the costumes from Hi-de-Hi! With a bit of clever make-up, Yvette made a perfect Peggy – Su Pollard would be proud of her! And as for Mark's Ted Bovis – even Joe Maplin would be fooled.

The series has ended now, but if the tales of Britain's worst Holiday Camp are ever repeated take a look at these photos and see if you can tell which Peggy and Ted are which!

Mark and Yvette are in the photo at the top of the page.

TO THE RESCUE

The Spirit of Grace Darling lives on!
This year marks the twenty-fifth anniversary of
Inshore Lifeboats and it is a special landmark for
all Blue Peter viewers, because the history of
lifeboats has become part of our history.

It was in May 1963 that the first Inshore Lifeboat
went on station. The launch was done very quietly,
because no-one knew if it was going to be a success.
The R.N.L.I. had always relied on the large traditional
boat to rescue people from shipwrecks. But now there
was a danger nearer at home. Holidaymakers were
taking to the water in small boats, inflatables
and air-beds, and they were doing it in their
thousands. A huge lifeboat needing a six man
crew was like taking a sledge hammer to
crack a nut.

A new, fast, shore-launched craft was
what was needed, and the new Inshore

*1963 – the first
Blue Peter
Lifeboats zoom
into action!
Viewers
collected
enough paperback books to
provide boats for Littlehampton,
Beaumaris, North Berwick
and St Agnes.*

50

Lifeboat was exactly that. Sixteen feet long, its tough nylon hull could bounce over the waves at twenty knots and its 2 man crew could get to the victim in minutes.

The new boat was an instant success, and seven more were assigned to stations at holiday resorts. By 1966 the R.N.L.I. knew that this was going to be a vital part of their services. But they desperately needed more boats.

Blue Peter viewers to the rescue!
Our Appeal in 1966 was for sixty thousand paperback books to provide one Inshore Lifeboat for Littlehampton in Sussex. We got books for three *more* boats which went to St Agnes in Cornwall, Beaumaris in Wales and North Berwick in Scotland.

But Inshore Lifeboats do not last forever and by 1972 North Berwick and St Agnes needed replacements and Littlehampton and Beaumaris had suitable launch sites for the new improved Atlantic 21 boats. When Blue Peter viewers take on a responsibility, they don't give it up easily and enough paperback books were sent to meet all requirements.

It was the same story in 1984 and this time we appealed for buttons and old postcards to provide four *more* replacements. In the end, we had enough for these, *plus* two extra.

These dramatic photos show Blue Peter IV trying to rescue people trapped by the tide.

The number of lives saved by the Blue Peter Inshore Lifeboats since we began in 1966 are:

		Launchings	Lives Saved
Blue Peter I	Littlehampton	785	245
Blue Peter II	Beaumaris	317	98
Blue Peter III	North Berwick	106	64
Blue Peter IV	St Agnes	251	118
Blue Peter V	Portaferry	16	2
		1,475	527

It is a sobering thought that the lives of five hundred and twenty-seven people have been saved because of Blue Peter viewers.

STOP PRESS!!
Blue Peter VI was provided as a result of our Double LifeSaver Appeal. It's a relief boat for any Lifeboat Station needing help.

YEAR OF THE DRAGON

What a sensational start to the Year of the Dragon with this red, scaley monster sneaking its way into the studio!

The Dragon is supposed to bring good luck by scaring away evil spirits and I should think just one look at our dragon's ferocious head, its huge white fangs and bulging eyes would have frightened anything to death!

Its colossal body – all forty-nine metres of it, was a series of bamboo cages, with brightly coloured material stretched over them. Each cage had a dancer holding it up– and when the body cloth was in position you only saw their legs and feet. During the dance, the tail has to do a fantastic amount of running, because it has to swish about more than any

other part of the body. So at least five tail runners are assigned to it and they swap places as the dance goes on.

There are five dancers who take turns holding the head, and they work hard, too.

I nearly collapsed when I had a go! It's very heavy, about two metres high and a metre wide with curling pink horns and great eyebrows and a beard made from sheepskin wool. It's got a large red tongue, too and during the dance, the great gaping jaws try to grab the Pearl – a sort of

30 pairs of legs powered the Dragon into the studio – with Bonnie chasing after them!

The dragon's giant gnashers try and grab a coloured ball, representing a pearl, during the dance.

The tail-carriers run the fastest of all the dancers!

Holding the head is no joke – it weighs a ton! During the procession, five dancers take it in turn to carry it, like a relay race. ▼

coloured ball on a long pole, held by another dancer, who weaves in and out of the crowd in front of the dragon, like an acrobat. At the beginning, the pearl, the most precious stone, is *inside* the Dragon and the greater the Dragon the larger the pearl. Then the Dragon spits it out and starts to play with the pearl – and the dance begins! And the climax of the dance is when once again the Dragon swallows the pearl.

One thing we couldn't do on Blue Peter was to get the whole Dragon to dance – the Chinese say it's very bad luck for this to happen before the actual day of the dance the Dragon's been made for. But fortunately the head separates from the body and we were told it was perfectly alright for the two parts to be moved individually.

By tradition, a band of musicians follow behind the tail of the Dragon and they beat out the rhythm so that all the Dragon's feet, right up to the head, dance in time. There's a complicated system sent from the tail, along the body to the head, to make sure the whole thing keeps in step – like everything else about the Dragon Dance, nothing was as simple as it seemed! As far as keeping evil spirits away – I'm not so sure. We had a lot of technical hitches in the studio that day. But maybe the magic didn't start until the following weekend, when the Dragon danced in Leicester Square, to the delight of

thousands of passers by.

Next February, the Chinese will be celebrating the Year of the Snake, so find out if there's going to be a Dragon dance near *you*. If you go along and have a look – you won't be disappointed. And like us, you can say "Kung Hey Fat Choy"! Happy New Year in Chinese!

53

RIGATONI CHICKEN

You can't beat pasta! Marathon runners and other athletes swear by it. Nourishing and cheap, there are thousands of recipes for all the different varieties – spaghetti, canelloni, lasagne, macaroni, rigatoni, penne, tagliatelle, fettucine, and loads more.

4 3 2 1

5

6

7

8

If you've never tried a pasta dish, why not start off with my Rigatoni Chicken?

Katie Bright who's six wrote to say:- "I cooked that recipe that you did on Monday's Blue Peter for Chicken Rigatoni. Mummy and I liked it very much. It was the first time I cooked lunch." If Katie can do it – so can you. Surprise *your* mum and cook her a meal fit for a Queen!

You will need:

50 grams or 2 oz butter or marge
50 grams or 2 oz flour
275 ml or ½ pint chicken stock
100 grams or 4 oz cooked chicken
100 grams or 4 oz sliced mushrooms (uncooked)
½ green pepper   chopped
½ red pepper   and
*   deseeded*
2 teaspoons of lemon juice
salt
freshly ground black pepper
¼ pint cream
250 grams or 8 oz Rigatoni
chopped parsley to garnish

Melt the butter or marge in a saucepan over a low heat and slowly blend in the flour. Mix well and stir constantly, for at least a minute (it's very important to keep stirring to get rid of all the lumps!). Add the chicken stock. Keep stirring and turn the heat up until the mixture boils and thickens. Take the saucepan off the heat and then add the cooked chicken, the sliced mushrooms and the chopped peppers. Mix well and add 2 teaspoons of lemon juice, a pinch of salt and some freshly ground pepper. Return the pan to the heat and simmer gently for 15 minutes. During this time, cook the rigatoni in a large saucepan of salted boiling water. When it's cooked (about 13–15 minutes) drain well in a colander and turn into a warmed serving dish. When the sauce is ready, for a touch of luxury stir in ¼ pint of single cream. Pour the sauce over the rigatoni and garnish with chopped parsley.

If you don't have any rigatoni you can use other pastas. Carrots, peas or sweetcorn can be used instead of peppers.

PASTA POWER

A bridge made out of Spaghetti? Forget it – I'm not *that* stupid! Most people would react like that if, like me, they were told Blue Peter was featuring not one but four bridges made from nothing but pasta. But it was true and here's how four of the finalists of the craziest challenge ever – the Spaghetti Bridge Building Competition – were put to the test.

1 Designed by 8 year old James Davies of Stoke-on-Trent, who hates spaghetti!
2 Entered by girls from Leeds High School.
3 The toughest bridge in our contest - built by 14 year old Robert Hillman.
4 The weakest bridge of our four finalists built by a team of 17 year olds from Sheffield.

The rules were simple – all contestants in the competition organised by the University of Leeds, had to use as *little* uncooked spaghetti as possible and their bridges had to be strong enough to carry the weight of 1 kilo or 2 lb 2 oz. Marks were also awarded for the design of the bridges, and it's amazing how different the bridges we tested looked.

On Blue Peter we devised a fiendish test that *wasn't* in the official Competition – a "Test to Destruction" – but in the end, the laugh was on us.

Try as we might – we couldn't break the bridges! As weight after weight was added two of them stood firm and strong. The item was lasting much too long – out of the corner of my eye, I could see the Floor Manager waving frantically, signalling to me we'd run out of time.

Finally, our contest was won by Robert Hillman of London whose bridge only buckled and snapped after we'd piled on a colossal two kilos of weights. Pasta Power's a force to be reckoned with!

Fourteen year-olds Vanessa Castle and Megan Anelay and 13 year old Joanna Newman from Leeds, were the only girls who made it to the Finals.

55

BONNIE'S "KEEP FIT"

Definitely not the best picture of me in this book as I try and coax Bonnie through Tony Veal's tunnel.

There's nothing Bonnie likes more than something new, especially if it's a real challenge. She's a very bright dog and the worst thing you can do with an alert animal is let it lie around and get lazy. That's why Bonnie and I started going to Agility classes. Bonnie seems to love them, but they leave me gasping for breath!

If you've ever watched Cruft's – the most famous dog show in the world – you might have seen the Junior Agility Classes. We've invited the winning team to the Blue Peter studio for the past two years, and their skill and co-ordination boggles your mind! It's not just the dogs – they're billiant of course – but the owners, too. They work just as hard as their pets, because it takes a lot of practice over a very long time

A tricky one this! Not so bad for a Scottie, but a handful for a Golden Retriever.

Up … and over! A lot of encouragement brings Bonnie over the jump.

to build up the sort of close link between animal and human that results in championships being won.

Seeing the dogs leap over, round and through our specially constructed obstacle course, I never dreamt that Bonnie and I could one day do the same thing. Well, so far we can't. But we're learning!

It all began with Richard Duckworth, the Devon-based dog trainer, who's done so much to help Bonnie – first with Janet when she was presenting Blue Peter, and more recently with me.

He always said what a very intelligent dog Bonnie is and that she could do more than she's generally asked to do on Blue Peter. Then, through Cruft's, we met all the dog agility enthusiasts. One of them – Tony Veal – who's appeared on the programme, offered to teach Bonnie and me at the regular classes he runs at Downe in Kent.

So we've started going, and let me tell you, there's a lot more to it than you'd imagine. For a start, there's a world of difference between saying a particular dog is intelligent, and actually getting her to perform. Bonnie can get over and round the obstacles – not very fast yet, but that's just a question of practice. But before she can be persuaded to perform at all, I have to get her excited enough to *want* to do it. So the training is very much for the human handler as well as the dog.

Walking the dog! Never done it a metre and a half off the ground before.

Superdog! She leaps wide ravines, swims mighty rivers ... or at least, she will do if she carries on at this rate!

No, Bonnie, you jump through the tyre. I'll watch

"More encouragement, it's all in your voice – much, much more praise, come *on* Yvette", shouts Tony, while Bonnie and I are making our way through a tyre or over a jump. Most of what he has to say is directed at me, not Bonnie. We've begun our training with Bonnie still on the lead, but I hope it won't be long before she's on her own and haring round the obstacles like the other dogs that go to Tony's classes. Trying to keep up with her is certainly helping to keep me fit!

And the main thing is that Bonnie really enjoys it. She's looking slimmer and more alert. It's terribly important to make sure your pet does as much as he or she is capable of – that way they'll lead a fuller, happier life, and you'll enjoy looking after them more. So if you've got a dog – you'd be surprised how many breeds are suitable – why not contact the nearest dog ability classes and take up the challenge. See you at Cruft's!

57

PICTURES IN THE POST

The Misses Westmorland Wood
C/o Commander A.W. WOOD RN
A 5 Bemloe,
Simla.
India.

There are two kinds of people: The neat and tidy ones who throw everything away the moment they've finished with it, because they hate clutter and like everything to be regular and ordered ... and the kind who can't bear to throw anything away.

They hoard things long after they've ceased to be useful. Their houses tend to be a bit of a clutter, and if you should open a drawer or a cupboard you would run the risk of being bombarded by an avalanche of junk. I'm on the side of the hoarders because if all the world had always

Some of the albums full of postcards and letters from the mysterious Kaka.

Kaka with one of his grandchildren –
Teddy
Westmorland
Wood.

Teddy and his sisters Ann, Margaret and Elizabeth – Kaka wrote to them all.

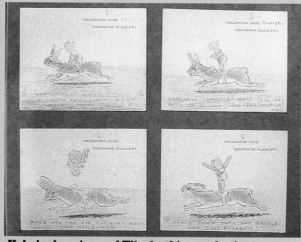

Kaka's drawings of Elizabeth's acrobatics must have surprised the Postman!

been neat and tidy our knowledge of the old days would have been very much poorer. This is a story of hoarders.

The first one was Mrs. Marion Grimaldi. Her son Charles had the enormous task of sorting all her possessions after she had died. It was, would you believe, five years after her death that Charles was going through an old wardrobe when his hands touched a strange object at the back. It didn't feel like clothes or shoes, and when he pulled it out he discovered it was a photograph album. It was covered in white linen and was very old and tatty. He opened it up, and to his

Hathi the Elephant and his friend Mr Hare were Kaka's favourite characters.

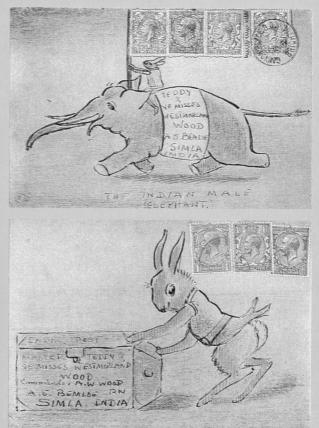

Lots of the cards and envelopes still have their old stamps and postmarks, which make them even more valuable collectors' items. Altogether Charles Grimaldi, Kaka's great grandson, tracked down eight hundred of them in six different albums.

surprise he discovered, not photographs, but page after page of postcards and letters and envelopes. They had all been hand written. But best of all, they were covered with the most marvellous drawings and cartoons. There were cats and dogs, birds, elephants and fish, and all kinds of strange mythical creatures as well. When Charles read the letters he discovered that they had been written to his mother when she was a little girl, living 7,000 miles away in India. But who had sent them?

When we asked Blue Peter viewers to let us know if they knew of any other letters from Kaka, we discovered two hundred and fifty more! They'd been sent to four other people – Katherine Richards. John Thornhill, William Jesse and Jeanne Montague-Brown.

They were all signed "Kaka", and Charles had never heard the name before in his life. Some people would have put the album back into the wardrobe and forgotten about it. But not Charles Grimaldi. He was fascinated by the letters, and by the mysterious writer, because the stories were told and the picture drawn with such dash and vigour – and such loving care – that the author must have been a truly outstanding person.

Charles' mother had two sisters who were now dead, and a brother who was still alive, so he wrote to his Uncle Teddy to ask if he could throw any light on the mysterious Kaka. Uncle Teddy replied. Kaka was the name he and his sisters had called their Grandfather. But there was even better news. 'Kaka' had written to Teddy as well, and he had *two* albums full of letters! Charles didn't leave it at that. If "Kaka" had written to his mother and his uncle, what about his two aunts … his mother's sisters Elizabeth and Ann? The hunt was on. Family attics were invaded. Fortunately everyone in the family seems to have been a hoarder, because when, at last an old tin trunk was opened, another *three* albums were discovered where they had lain for an incredible sixty years. Altogether, he found six albums containing eight hundred letters and cards. The collection is so unusual that it has been estimated to be worth a staggering £250,000!

Kaka turned out to have been a very distinguished soldier whose real name was Sir Henry Thornhill. He had spent many years in India himself and was fascinated by its birds and animals. A friend of his said: "There was not one bird he couldn't tell you about … plumage … call … nesting habits. He could even imitate the calls of birds," Animals and birds feature prominently in his drawings.

He began by writing to Teddy from the age of one and a half onwards. As soon as the girls reached eighteen months he started to send them postcards, and then when they were five he changed to proper letters which were lavishly illustrated. He wrote to each child once a fortnight over a period of five years.

Now for the most amazing news. It has been discovered that Kaka wrote to many other children … outside the family! Children who

Katherine Richards with her older sisters – Gwynedd, Audrey and Enid.

were ill in hospital. None of these letters has so far been discovered, but let's hope that the people he wrote to turned out to be hoarders too, because somewhere there could be a rich quarry of Kaka

▲ *As Kaka grew older his style changed. He drew more pictures in pen and ink – like this large lady taking her dog for a walk.*

letters mouldering in some old attic. By now we had been bitten by the same bug as Charles and decided to join in the great "Kaka" letters hunt. So we asked you to help us. "Do you know of anyone who has written letters with drawings in them like this?" we asked on the programme. Never ask "Blue Peter" viewers for something if you don't want a positive result! It was overwhelming. We had hoped that perhaps one or two letters might turn up. What did we get – two hundred and fifty! Some of the letters came from as far away as Switzerland and America. It is amazing, when you think of the care which went into each drawing, that Kaka, in a busy and successful career, had found the time to do them.

He continued to write and draw for children into his old age. We discovered some letters sent to a child in Switzerland where Kaka had retired when he became ill. In one of them he wrote:

"My head is fuzzy wuzzy, and my fingers refuse to write and draw what I ask them … so I won't fight anymore".

When Teddy was an undergraduate at Cambridge he wrote to Kaka in Switzerland: "If we do not meet again in this world, Kaka dear, we will meet someday in the happy hunting grounds". Happy hunting grounds was a favourite Kaka expression. Kaka died in Switzerland in 1942. He was eighty nine years old.

THE PANDAS' INCREDIBLE JOURNEY

Everyone loves the beautiful giant panda. It has been made the badge of the World Wild Life Fund. But fifty years ago, no one in the west had seen a giant panda alive.

Floyd Tangier Smith, who was known as the Gentle Hunter, decided to try to bring one panda *ALIVE* to Europe. This was a great breakthrough. Other hunters hardly cared if they brought out the pandas alive or dead.

Tangier Smith had a special way of trapping pandas, and his secret was *SUGAR*! His assistant Lin laid a trail of sugar lumps from the bamboo forest to a clearing, where Tangier Smith and his assistants waited to lassoo the pandas and slip them into cages. In three amazing days, they caught *FIVE* pandas!

Then a small cub walked out of the jungle, straight into Tangier Smith's arms. Now he really had a problem.

In the wild, giant pandas only eat bamboo. Tangier Smith calculated: *"It will take about nine weeks to get to England. We shall need 37,000 pieces of bamboo"*. So the assistants started cutting.

Tangier Smith bought forty-two mules to carry the mountains of bamboo, but before they could get started, *TWO MORE* pandas wandered into the camp. *"It was as if an incredible miracle crossed our path. If six is a record, eight must surely be unbeatable!"*

After three days on mountain tracks they reached the town of CHENGDU. The whole town turned out to welcome them, in streets decorated with twenty thousand Chinese lanterns. Tangier Smith, calling out *"Make way for the holy pandas"*, presented the delighted mayor of the town with the last two pandas to join the expedition.

Each panda was measured and given a name. The first four were called MING, CHANG, TANG and SUNG, but the last two had different names. That day was the 88th birthday of the grandmother of Tangier Smith's valued assistant, Lin. *"We will pay our respects to your honourable grandmother, and name the last two pandas 'GRANDMA' and 'HAPPY'"*.

The expedition must have been an amazing sight, as for twenty-four days it moved on slowly, stopping for the pandas to take a dip in the rivers, or have a walk, on leads like dogs. *"They have become the children of my life, nothing has so enriched my life as their presence!"*

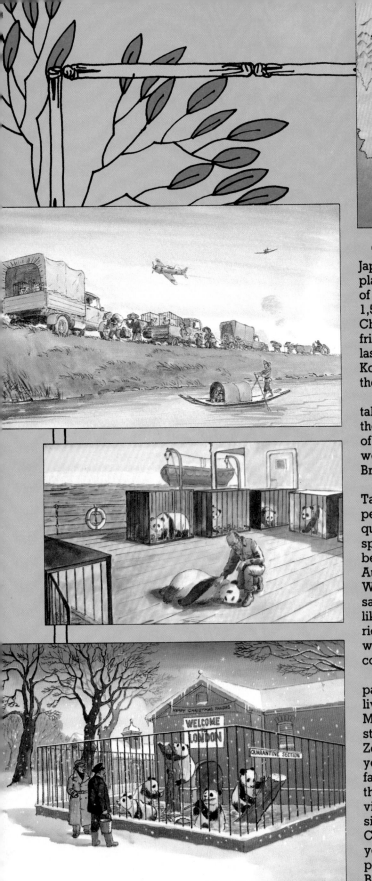

The journey was fraught with danger. Japan was at war with China, and enemy planes bombed them. They found a convoy of battered army trucks to take them the next 1,500 agonising miles through war-torn China to the coast. The pandas were very frightened, and went right off their food. At last they reached the British colony of Hong Kong. All six pandas were still alive … but they had another ten thousand miles to go.

They found the S.S. Antenor was ready to take them on their journey to England. On the voyage Chang, the biggest panda died of seasickness, but the rest did well, and six weeks after leaving China, they reached Britain.

It was Christmas, 1938. The pandas were Tangier Smith's Christmas present to the people of Britain! Soon they were in their quarters at London Zoo, were they would spend six months in quarantine. They had been travelling for four months, since August, and now it was Christmas Eve. When they looked out of their cages, and saw the snow lying thick on the ground, just like in the mountains of China, and ate the rice gruel and fresh bamboo that was waiting for them, the pandas felt they had come home at last.

The other pandas did not live long, but Ming was the star of London Zoo for six years, and fascinated thousands of visitors. And since that Christmas, fifty years ago, the people of Britain have loved the rare, shy, beautiful giant panda.

Even Princess Elizabeth, now The Queen, visited Ming.

救救熊猫！

FLYING FINN

It was a case of "blink and you'll miss it" the day thirteen year old Zoe Finn came to the studio. Zoe has only been trampolining for three years, but she's a star! She already held the record for performing the most somersaults on a trampoline in one minute, when she came to see us intending to break it once again. The record stood at *seventry-three* somersaults. Caron and Yvette both had to have a go at trampolining during their Blue Peter auditions, so they know how difficult it is to do just *one* somersault, but to Zoe they're like water off a duck's back.

One reason for her success is the fact that she's very small. As you can see from the multiple-image picture she manages to keep her head virtually still while she's jumping. Zoe told us if she was going to break her own record she'd have to do it fast, before she got too big to attempt it.

WELL DONE, ZOE!

The main picture of Zoe was taken by photographer Philip Carr. He used a Mamiya RB67 camera with ASA 400 film, and a stroboscopic light flashing 12 times each second.

So with her coach Martin Laws standing by, and with a scrutineer from the Guinness Book of Records – it was an official attempt on a World Record – Zoe went for it. She flew through the air at the rate of more than *one somersault a second*, with Martin counting them out, so Zoe could pace herself and not burn up too soon.

We all held our breath as the seconds ticked by and the somersaults mounted up ... past thirty, over forty, approaching fifty. Then suddenly the old record of seventy-three was in sight.

Zoe sailed past it, with four seconds left on the clock. Then with a final burst of energy she went even faster at the very end, finishing up with seventy-eight somersaults. That's a record that Zoe will never break herself. But, who knows, it may be shattered one day – and we hope it'll be done in the Blue Peter studio.

Say it with Flowers

Here's how you can have roses all the year round – and they'll never fade or die!

Paper roses are easy to make and they're the perfect present for special occasions like Mothering Sunday, when flowers in the shops are expensive. You can make a whole bunch or just a few roses in a gold presentation box. You can even make your own vases, too!

1 TO MAKE THE ROSES:

From one packet of crepe paper you should be able to make at least a dozen roses. Start by cutting a length from the short side of the roll. There's no need to measure anything. Try and keep it straight but don't worry if it goes a bit wobbly. Fold the cut out length of crepe paper in half, then half again so it's roughly square, then cut the folded edges, off. You will now have lots of loose squarish pieces – these are the petals.

1 ▶

3 Pick the pieces up altogether and fold them in half so that the green piece is on the outside. Then roll them into a cone shape and you can see them magically turn into a rose.

3 ▶

YOU WILL NEED:
Coloured crepe paper (red, pink, white or any colour you choose).
Green sticky tape. Green card.
Green garden sticks or dowel rods.
Rubber solution glue.
Plastic margarine tub or Plastic bottle or Yoghurt pot or Cereal packet.
Silver sticky tape. Ribbon.

2
Lay the crepe squares on top of each other – on the squint – to make them look like petals.

If you have any green paper, you can cut an extra smaller square to make the flower a little more real-looking where it's going to join the stalk. But if you haven't any green paper don't worry, the rose will still look alright.

Lay the green square on top of the pile.

2 ▼

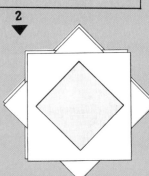

66

4
Fasten the rose tightly with green sticky tape or paint clear tape green.

Then bend the crepe paper down to make the petals look just like the real thing.

If you want to make buds or little roses for small pots, all you have to do is make the paper squares smaller.

4a ▶

4b ▶

4c ▶

5
THE STEMS
The stems are green garden sticks. The roses look pretty if they are of different lengths. So from one stick you can get one long and one short stem or three short stems. They cut quite easily with scissors. Now all you have to do is wind a piece of sticky tape round the flower and the stem to hold them together.

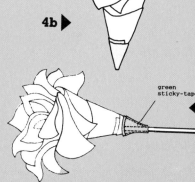

green
sticky-tape

◀ **5**

6 THE LEAVES
For a finishing touch it's well worth adding leaves. First make a pattern, just a simple leaf shape that you can mark out on green card.

◀ **6a**

◀ **6b**

Now draw round the pattern on to green card – you'll need about twenty of these shapes for a bowlful.

When you've cut them out, score down the centre of each leaf with a bradawl, or a knitting needle, and then bend them slightly along the lines to give them a proper rose leaf look.

Make a hole with the bradawl in the bottom of the leaf – this is where the stem will slide through.

◀ **7 FIXING LEAVES**
Put a dab of rubber solution glue on the right side of the hole and slide it on to the stem. Press the leaf firmly in place under the rose.

dab of glue

THE VASE
If you have got plenty of long sticks, you might like to make a vase to hold tall roses. Caron used a plastic bottle, cut the neck off, painted it and finished it off with a silver trim of sticky tape.

THE SMALL POT
The little pot for rose buds is just a painted yoghurt pot, and, to hold the buds in place, Caron stuck them into a lump of modelling clay placed inside the pot.

THE BOWL
The silver bowl started life as a plastic margarine tub. Wash it well, make some holes in the lid to hold the rose stems, then replace the lid. When you've painted it – any colour looks nice – you will find that you can make a very pretty display by putting the taller flowers in the centre and the shorter ones around the edge.

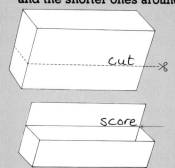

cut ✂

score

THE PRESENTATION BOX
Just a few roses can make a very glamorous present. The gold presentation box started life as a Cornflake packet. Cut one side off and leave a flap for the lid. Score down the flap to make a hinge, then paint the box. When it is dry glue on a piece of ribbon for a finishing touch.

67

FLIGHT FANTASTIC

The elegant Harriet Quimby, who flew the Channel in a Bleriot monoplane (right).

Boyish Amelia Earhart set many aviation records in the 1930s.

Bet you've never heard of Harriet Quimby! If you'd been around seventy-five years ago, you would have done.

Harriet was one of the great pioneers of aviation. She was an American with a burning ambition – to become the first woman to fly the English Channel!

Her aeroplane had only as much power as the smallest motorbike you could buy today, and looked more like a fragile insect than what we think of as a plane. But Harriet wasn't afraid. She was so eager to make the flight, she didn't even have a practice first. She took off from Kent at dawn on April 16th 1912, with a hot water bottle to keep her warm.

Harriet couldn't see a thing because it was foggy, but after twenty minutes, through the mist, she saw land ahead. As carefully as she could, she landed her little plane. She was in France!

Sadly, Harriet Quimby did not live long to enjoy her fame. She was killed in a flying accident when she was only twenty-eight.

As more and more aviation records were set throughout the 1920s, the pilots became stars, none bigger than Charles Lindbergh, the American who in 1927 achieved what seemed to be the ultimate flight – across the Atlantic, alone. Lindbergh's fame inspired another American who set out to become just as famous with an even longer flight.

Her name was Amelia Earhart, who soon achieved a reputation as a

Harriet signing autographs soon after she landed in France. Out of her flying gear (far right), she was the model of an Edwardian gentlewoman.

Amelia at the controls of her beloved Lockheed Electra in 1937.

Amelia's companion on the round-the-world flight was Captain Fred Noonan. This snap was taken during the trip, when they reached Brazil.

daredevil pilot. She started planning something that no man or woman had ever done. She intended to fly *right round the world* with just one companion, a navigator. There would be many stops because in those days planes could only fly a couple of thousand miles without refuelling. But even so, this would be an achievement beyond comparison – if she managed it.

With Fred Noonan, the navigator, she took off in her Lockheed Electra on May 20th 1937. She left from California, flying east. Everything went well in the long and arduous flight all the way through America, Africa, Asia and out across the Pacific. From Northern Australia, they began one of the longest legs of their marathon, to Howland Island a dot in the ocean 2,500 miles away. It was a treacherous flight, through tropical storms, and requiring pinpoint navigation. The United States Navy stationed ships along the way, to pick up radio messages from Amelia. The last one they received said, "Our gas is running low". Amelia was never heard from again. The fabulous Amelia Earhart, first lady of the skies, was dead.

Throughout the history of flight, there have been brave women like Harriet Quimby and Amelia Earhart, who have stretched the boundaries of endurance, testing both their planes and themselves against the toughest conditions. Amy Johnson became the pride of Britain after her solo flight to Australia in 1930. Another Briton, Sheila Scott, flew right round the Equator, 32,000 gruelling miles in 1966.

All these brave women have laid the foundations for the women that follow them today – the women who at long last are taking their rightful place behind the controls of the world's biggest and most advanced airliners.

Blue Peter's latest woman of the skies – Caron airborne on a cloud-hopper at a hot air balloon event in the Alps.

CARON'S CLOTHES

Caron's outfits have raised many eyebrows. "I've never wanted to wear clothes that you might see other people in," she says. "And I don't believe people want to see ordinary clothes they might find anywhere, when they watch television."

Her individual style has won her many admirers. It's always a

"The producers should do something about Caron Keating's dress sense. She would be better employed in the Blue Peter garden – keeping the birds away!"

We've had lots of letters like those. Thankfully, we've also had lots like this.

"We are always trying to copy Caron's clothes, she looks brilliant."

moment to look forward to, just before our dress rehearsal, when Caron appears in the outfit she's going to wear for the show. Sometimes the producers have trouble working out what it is, or where one part ends and another starts, but by and large, they agree with her fans – Miss Caron Keating is one of the most stylish stars on TV!

You won't be surprised to learn that Caron loves shopping. "I spend a lot of time shopping, and don't miss an opportunity. If there's a spare hour when I'm filming, I'm off to the nearest High Street."

Markets are a favourite haunt – that's where Caron picks up a lot of second-hand clothes cheaply.

If you see a familiar jacket or skirt that went to a jumble sale turning up on Blue Peter, don't be too surprised – Caron's worn many cast-offs that she's found around the country. "I used to go to the Oxfam shops, but so many people know about them these days, that most of the good stuff gets snapped up too quickly."

"My favourite colours at the moment are green, white and black – especially black. The trouble is, even if I love a particular outfit, I can't wear it more than a few times on television because viewers *do* remember what they've seen me in. I try to mix and match, of course, but I do get through a lot of clothes."

When she'd not doing Blue Peter, you'll probably find Caron in a very scruffy pair of jeans, with knees worn through (they're not "designer" holes!), a simple t-shirt and a black jumper. "I like to be as comfortable as possible. If some people think I look scruffy on the programme, they should see me at home!"

POWER to the PEOPLE

As this 1930s cover of a boys' magazine shows, Battersea was the symbol of the engineering genius of the age.

It's funny how we British get so fond of the oddest things – brown sauce, the weather and Roland Rat, to name but three. Over the last fifty years, Londoners have grown very attached to four enormous chimneys that have belched smoke over the city and a pile of eight million bricks that have dominated a stretch of the River Thames skyline. When it was announced that Battersea Power Station was finally to close, what could be more typically British than slapping a preservation order on all those bricks? That left a dead power station that couldn't be knocked down but whose days of producing electricity were over.

Along comes the answer in the form of a smooth, rich businessman who could have stepped right out of the screen in an old British film. But this is where the story stops being British and leaps off into Disneyworld. The businessman, John Broome, plans to spend three years turning the turbines, boilers and generators of Battersea into a pleasure park – a fun palace with rides, cinemas, theatres, restaurants, even an ice rink. "There'll be nothing like it on the planet," he told Caron, in a very un-British boast.

Caron visited Battersea as the last of its station innards were being wrenched out. There were once seventeen boilers blasting away, producing the heat from which electricity for a very large part of London was made. When Caron filmed amid the sparks of blow-torches in the old boiler room, there were just two-and-a-half of the old monsters left. It was the same story in the turbine room – now just an empty hall. Workmen have spent years cutting up and carting away what was once the pride of British engineering genius.

Many eyebrows have been raised by the idea of turning a power station into

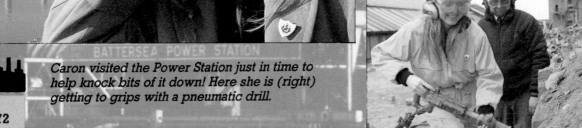

Caron visited the Power Station just in time to help knock bits of it down! Here she is (right) getting to grips with a pneumatic drill.

The massive Turbine Hall in 1933 (above) and the same Turbine Hall today (top right). The giant machines have gone as Battersea awaits its next life as a pleasure palace.

The control room shows the attention that went into Battersea – marble, stainless steel and a hardwood floor.

Much of its fame is due to the architect, Giles Gilbert Scott. He's more famous as the man who designed Liverpool's Anglican Cathedral. At Battersea, he turned his skills to designing a Cathedral of Power. He was called in once the steel framework containing the guts of the power station was already up. He introduced many of the features which made Battersea so unusual. He softened the look of the outside by using the bricks – incidentally, they're just for decoration. They're not actually holding the place up. Scott designed the fluted columns of brick, which gave the chimneys their famous tapered look. Inside, the power station looked more like a 1930s dance floor than the kind of grimy place you might expect. The cabinets in the control room were all made out of expensive stainless steel, the walls were Italian marble, the floor was polished hardwood. In the words of one ex-station manager: "You weren't allowed to walk in there unless you put felt overshoes on. You could literally eat off it."

Don't suppose anyone dared!

an amusement park but arguments over Battersea are nothing new. In the 1920s and 1930s, they argued about whether it should be built, what it should look like, and complained about the tons of stinking, sulphurous smoke dumped on the capital each year. In fact, the chemists at Battersea did a great deal of valuable research in "washing" the gases that went up Battersea's chimneys, taking the sulphur fumes out. Gradually the massive chimneys on the Thames (only two at first – the other two were added when the second half, Battersea 'B' was built in the 1940s. In reality, Battersea is *two* power stations) became familiar and friendly landmarks. Royalty and VIPs visited and eventually Battersea became more than just a power station. Its sheer size, the never-ending list of impressive and record-breaking facts about its work, its unusual artistic design – all these things turned it into a highlight of London, as much part of the city as St Paul's Cathedral and Tower Bridge.

Those days are gone, of course. If the plans for Battersea are turned into reality, the power station is setting out on a journey just as remarkable as its past. After fifty years of providing electricity for millions of Londoners Battersea can look forward to many years of playing host to the people of the capital as a centre of entertainment. Who would have guessed, fifty years ago, that one day Battersea's "consumption" and "production" would be measured not in millions of tons of coal and thousands of megawatts of electricity, but in candyfloss, popcorn and laughter?

The man behind the transformation – John Broome, with a model of his Battersea dream.

Anyone who remembers me zooming up into the air at the Moscow State Circus, will know I'm not frightened of a challenge. But when I went rafting in Bala, the watersports centre in North Wales, I ran out of steam. I was there with a bunch of sixteen and seventeen year olds from London, who were training for an expedition to the Himalayan Mountain

kingdom of Nepal. The team planned to take their own canoes and rafts to travel down or ford the rivers in their path. In Nepal, the rivers are wide, rocky and rough, a test for the best canoeists.

 Snowdonia might not be the Himalayas, but the rivers are no

We tried to paddle together in the raft, so that when we hit the roughest water we'd have the raft well under control ...

... but it didn't do the slightest good! Going over the rapids knocked us sideways, and left the crew looking a shambles.

My first canoeing experience on the river didn't last long. I was soon out of the kayak, gasping for breath and soaked to the skin.

picnic, especially if your canoeing experience runs to one evening's practice in a swimming pool. Fortunately, the Nepal team knew quite a bit more about canoes than that, so they showed me how to tackle the rapids. They shot down the river, skillfully using the current to skim past the rocks and dipping their paddles with the grace of artists using their paintbrushes to keep their balance. I didn't find it so easy!

It felt more like sitting on a bar of soap in the bath. It wasn't surprising I tipped over once or twice and became very familiar with the *underwater* view of the river! Luckily I'd been taught righting drill by one of the expedition leaders, Mickie Gordon.

The team's also taking inflatable rafts, each crewed by six paddlers, to Nepal. I took to the water with one of the loudest of the team members right behind the raft.

Melanie wasn't going to allow me a moment's rest – "It's so rough, this river," I gasped, between facefuls of water.

"Shut up Yvette, keep paddling," was the only reply. "Paddle on the right, PADDLE ON THE RIGHT," yelled Melanie as our raft began to turn in a gentle circle and present its rear end to the next set of rapids!

Eventually, with a good deal more of the River Tryweryn *inside* the raft than there seemed to be left in the river, we reached the calmer water of the shallows. We'd made it – I never thought we would!

Cold, soaking and sneezing, I'd definitely had enough of the river. The canoeing was actually very frightening, and I was only able to attempt it because experts like Mike Coyne, a vastly experienced Himalayan backpacker, were on hand to get me out of trouble. I wouldn't mind a holiday in Nepal. But by canoe? Forget it!

Under Mickey Gordon's instruction, I tried again Balancing the canoe wasn't made any easier by having a film camera strapped on.

Team Leader Mick Coyne will have his hands full in Nepal – but at least he won't have me to worry about!

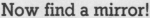

SOLUTIONS

Now find a mirror!

6 Victoria, the Robot Cow, invented by Adrian Wareham, has a petrol powered 50 cc engine and can walk at seven miles per hour.

7 These metal suits are replicas of the armour worn by King Henry VIII, on display at the Tower of London.

8 Zoidzilla! A colossal motorized model of the comic strip monster.

9 This rare albino hedgehog came to the studio with some other animals rescued by Les and Sue Stocker and cared for at St Tiggywinkles – their hedgehog hospital.

10 Inside the campaign caravan used by Field Marshall Viscount Montgomery of Alamein, who led the British 8th Army to victory in North Africa in the Second World War.

Puzzle Pictures

1 Bonnie meets Fat Pig – star of a new musical, with his backing group, the Hot Bananas band.

2 This brilliant Dalek car was made by Percy Watkins from bits and pieces of a Mini, parts of an Allegro and a scrapped Austin 1100!

3 We recreated the studio of the artist who painted "matchstick men and matchstick dogs and cats" – L. S. Lowry. He drew the sketch Mark's holding when he was twelve years old.

4 Richard Rutt – Bishop of Leicester started knitting when he was seven. He's created hundreds of garments, rugs and toys – including his own Bishop's hat, a mitre!

5 Hooray for Hollywood! Mark and Caron dressed up as two famous film stars, Mickey Rooney and Judy Garland, for our Christmas spectacular.

Useful information

Grace Darling Appeal
RNLI, West Quay Road, Poole, Dorset BH15 1HZ.

Grace Darling Museum
Radcliffe Road, Bamburgh, Northumberland NE69 7AE.
Open daily from 17th April until 30th September 11 a.m. – 6 p.m. During June, July and August open until 7 p.m.

Riding for the Disabled Association
Avenue R, National Agricultural Centre, Kenilworth, Warwickshire CV8 2LY.

Intourist Moscow Limited
292 Regent Street, London W1R 6QL.
Telephone: 01-631 1252.

RSPB's South Stack Reserve
Holyhead, Isle of Anglesey, Gwynedd, North Wales.

The Fabulous Panda by Michael de Havilland
Published by Pan Books   Price £4.95.

St Tiggywinkles
The Wildlife Hospital Trust
1 Pemberton Close, Aylesbury, Bucks HP21 7NY.
Telephone: (0296) 29860.

The Complete Hedgehog by Les Stocker
Published by Chatto & Windus
Price £6.95.

Pictures in the Post
The Illustrated Letters of Sir Henry Thornhill to his Grandchildren
Edited by Michael Baker
Published Bantam Press   Price £14.95.

A part of the proceeds from the sale of this book will be donated to the Save The Children Fund.

Dog Agility Classes
Further information on Kennel Club Junior Organisation can be obtained from:
Mr Tony Veal
Laburnum, Hollywood Lane, West Kingsdown, Kent TN15 6JG.
Don't forget to enclose a stamped addressed envelope!

National White Water Centre
Frongoch, Bala, Gwynedd LL23 7NU.
Telephone: 0678 520826

Women of the Air
by Judy Lomax
Published by John Murray   Price £11.95.

Acknowledgements

Co-ordinator: *Anne Dixon*
Designed by: *Judy Billson*
Typeset by: *DP Photosetting, Aylesbury, Bucks*
Production: *Landmark Production Consultants Ltd, London*
Colour separation by: *Fotographics Ltd, London & Hong Kong*
Heroine of the Seas and Flight Fantastic were written by *Dorothy Smith.*
The Panda's Incredible Journey was retold by *Dorothy Smith* from the book *The Fabulous Panda* by *Michael de Havilland*, published by Pan Books Ltd.
The Panda's Incredible Journey was illustrated by *Robert Broomfield.*

Personal Organisers and Say It With Flowers by K. S. Video.

Photographs were taken by
Barry Lewis/Radio Times, Robert Hill, John Jefford, John Green, Phil Taylor, Dave Edwards, Peter Lane, Chris Capstick, Joan Williams, Philip Carr, Tim Roney, George Pope, Julian Calder, Steve Nichols, Anthony Reynolds LBIPP LMPA, Lewis Bronze, Nicholas Heathcote,
RSPB/W. W. Richards and *C. H. Gomersall*
The authors and publishers wish to thank the following for providing illustrative material: *BBC Hulton Picture Library; The Smithsonia Institution, Washington, DC; The Keystone Collection; C.E.G.B.; British Gas; R.N.L.I.; Mrs Connie Thrower; J. E. J. Whitaker, Charles Grimaldi and John Frost Newspapers.*

Blue Peter COMPETITION

Would you like to come to the Television Centre and see the Blue Peter studio? Would you like to meet the Blue Peter team and all the animals?

This could be your chance to come to London and meet them all at a special party!

This photo was taken during one of Bonnie's Agility Classes. Write not more than twenty words telling us what *you* think Bonnie might have been thinking!

The twenty people who send us the best suggestions will be invited to our BLUE PETER PARTY.

The closing date is January 31st 1989. Cut out your entry and send it to:

Blue Peter Competition
BBC Television Centre
London W12 7RJ

First prize winners and runners-up will be notified by letter.

Age ....

Name ....

Address ....

Bonnie was thinking ....

77